A Mother's Journey

KERRY ALDERUCCIO

LOVE&WRITE
PUBLISHING

This is a book dedicated to you, my beautiful son, Sam, and also to my wonderful dad, Jim Bell, and to all of you in the spirit world.

A heartfelt thank you to all of Sam's incredible friends and to our respective families, who have all supported us emotionally and in so many other amazing ways.

Thank you to my husband, Sergio, and daughter, Carla, for believing in me every step of the way in my unplanned yet fully pre-mapped journey.

Dare to believe …

A Love & Write book
PO Box 252
Summer Hill NSW 2130
Australia

www.loveandwrite.com.au

Copyright text © Kerry Alderuccio, 2018
Copyright design © Love & Write Publishing, 2018

All rights reserved. No part of this publication may be reproduced, stored in a retrieval system or transmitted in any form or by any means, electronic, mechanical, photocopying, recording or otherwise, without the prior written permission of the publisher.

A copy of this publication can be found in the National Library of Australia.

Edited by Lisa Macken
Designed by Jessica Le, Love & Write Publishing

Printed in Australia

ISBN 978-1-925564-25-9

10 9 8 7 6 5 4 3 2 1

Contents

	Introduction	vii
1.	Who we are	1
2.	About Sam	25
3.	The accident	43
4.	The days after	51
5.	Funeral and memorial services	59
6.	Moving forward	71
7.	The lights at Farnham Street	77
8.	Dreams and visits	81
9.	Seeing a medium	85
10.	Hope … and getting back to living	95
11.	Moving house	101
12.	Signs and messages	111
13.	Graffiti tags and stories	121
14.	Sitting in circle	125
15.	My turning point	133
16.	The importance of celebrating birthdays and anniversaries	155
17.	Where we are now	171

Introduction

It would be fair to ask yourself at this very early stage: 'Why am I reading this book?', but there is no plain, simple or uncomplicated answer to this question. I can only assume that you, like me, have also had to endure the agony of losing a child or loved one. All passings are tragedies in their own right: finding a way to cope and somehow move forward seems to be something that not enough is written about.

This is my first book. Never for a moment did I think that I would be writing about something so personal and tragic as the passing of our son, Sam, in a horrific car accident on 3 May 2012. Sam did not pass on his own; two of his best mates, Raph and Jesse, were also with him and three beautiful souls were lost to this world that day. Three families were directly affected and many more were also stricken as the domino effect took hold and the realisation of what happened was fully grasped. The topic is not of my choosing, but in life you don't always get to choose.

It is true to say that nothing prepares you for the loss of a child. It is usually totally unexpected and it certainly destroys the naturally perceived order of family succession. Not only do parents lose a child, but siblings lose their friend and first playmate. Life from here on is never truly complete, the void cannot be filled and the physical absence is always so painful and apparent.

For those of you who have experienced this indescribable pain and deep sense of loss, I hope so very much that our story will somehow help you deal with your own grief in a way that will ideally offer you a feeling of hope for the future, and a way of dulling the pain of today.

I truly wish that a book such as this one existed when Sam passed, because all I wanted was simple answers to seemingly impossible questions such as: 'Where has Sam actually gone and is he okay?' It is my intention that some of your own questions will be answered as a direct result of me sharing our story, and my greater *hope* that you will be left feeling just that ... **hope.**

In order to share our story properly and for it to make sense, I have decided to start at the most obvious place: at the very beginning.

CHAPTER 1

Who we are

My husband, Sergio, and I first met in 1972 when we were the worldly age of twelve, as we both embarked on our formative high school years at the newly opened, but yet to be built, high school at Mooroopna in country Victoria. Secondary school for us was six years spent in a dry and inhospitable paddock being schooled in portable classrooms for the first two years, and then to more permanent accommodation that was continually being constructed over our remaining four years.

Our first real classrooms had barely been completed and opened when a huge flood in May 1974 claimed the off-white coloured carpet and everything else that sat upon it. We went without floor coverings until new and rather hideous rust-coloured carpet could be afforded and duly laid about a year later.

Both Sergio and I were oblivious to having a total lack of normal high school facilities, such as a gymnasium, a canteen (this came in our third year), proper toilet blocks, an auditorium or specifically built classrooms for photography, woodwork, science, home economics and so on. We just considered it all to be a great new adventure.

We are both outgoing by nature and jointly loved meeting newfound friends and having these unique experiences at Mooroopna High. Character building to say the least, and to us both seemingly perfectly normal at the same time.

I was a 'townie' from Tatura, or 'Tat' as the locals called it. My parents were very dedicated to their small family, just my older sister Susan and myself, and both were from hard-working stock. My dad, Jim, was a self-employed builder, starting out originally as a carpenter and then branching out to larger construction projects of a civil engineering nature. His work often took him away from home for weeks at a time, but Mum and Dad both knew that this sacrifice was crucial if they were to build a much sought-after nest egg and better way of life for the family.

My mum, Joan, worked in the office of the local veterinary clinic. She also often managed to be present to assist in theatre when the vets performed operations on smaller domestic animals at the surgery, which she loved doing. Mum worked over the years in various other local businesses, including one of the two chemist shops in town, and at the local newspaper, where she was sometimes the photographer and author of small articles. She later became a local councillor and was always extremely adaptable to any task at hand.

Mum, Susan, me and Dad in 1976

Sergio was from the more sparsely populated farming town and associated rural area called Toolamba, where his family worked extremely hard in the summer heat growing and picking tomatoes, and raising beef cattle. For quite a time Sergio's dad, Salvatore, or Sam as he preferred to be known, also had a small fleet of Commer trucks that transported the picked tomato crops to the fruit markets in Melbourne.

Sergio's dad and mum emigrated from Sicily in 1948 and 1958 respectively, after Sam went back to his homeland to marry his beautiful bride, Maria, in a pre-arranged wedding celebration. The plan was then to bring Maria to Australia, where everything just happened to be the geographical and cultural opposite of everything she knew in Sicily. It was how things were done then and the hardships of making these drastic changes are almost impossible to imagine. Together they worked tirelessly on the land and raised three children on the farm: Sergio, Robert and Diana.

Although Sergio and I were always firm friends throughout our high school years, our romantic relationship was one that got off to a very, very slow start. We started dating one another, aged twenty-nine, after catching up again at a high school reunion the year before back in Mooroopna, where it all began. After numerous beers and boisterous conversation at the Cricketers Arms Hotel, Sergio decided to give me his business card, which I wisely filed away for another time.

Not long after the school reunion I finally decided to move to the 'big smoke' to enjoy all that Melbourne had to offer.

After ten years working as a customer service officer for Medibank Private, I decided to sell my weatherboard Californian bungalow house in Shepparton. I was fortunate enough to receive a transfer to the overseas claims section of Medibank Private at head office in Bourke Street in September 1988. I loved my new life in Melbourne and embraced city living to the full. My world was shared with two cats, Woolley and Slate, who illegally moved with me into my crammed rented flat in Brunswick West. Heady and exciting stuff indeed!

As my first New Year's Day in Melbourne dawned, for no particular reason I felt that the time was right to retrieve the business card from my wallet and phone Sergio to let him know that I had finally made the big move from Shepparton. A dinner date immediately followed at the iconic and still operating Copperwood Restaurant in Lygon Street, Carlton: possibly the strangest dining choice imaginable, because unbeknown to us there was a regular Saturday night dinner dance happening. When you are still in your twenties dinner dances are not necessarily where you want to be; regardless, we had a fantastic night and shared further dinners in other, more exciting and age-appropriate locations.

We started to spend as much time as possible together and things progressed quite quickly on all levels. I began working for Sergio at his company, Franchise Developments, near the city on St Kilda Road. Sergio had begun the business from scratch some six years earlier, as a very driven and eager to succeed twenty-three year old.

Interacting with people and sales was always a passion of mine, although previously it was limited to processing medical and hospital claims and selling health insurance premiums, however, I began my newfound career with Sergio's company with the impressive sounding title of franchisee selection manager. At the time there were so many huge life changes happening, and it was still only one month after we had reconnected in January. As they say, there is no time like the present.

Our romantic relationship together was intentionally kept firmly under wraps, with no one at work being aware that we were dating. This was until November 1989, when an untimely and almost catastrophic motorbike accident on Sergio's beloved Harley-Davidson put an end to our covert relationship. The obvious question was then being asked: 'Why was Kerry with Sergio on his motorbike?' The proverbial cat was out of the bag!

Our days of secretive yet fantastic outings with the Melbourne chapter of Harley Owners Group, or HOG as they preferred to be known, all came to a very sticky end after an impatient farmer and his wife turned in front of our bike then panicked and stopped their ute, blocking our path on the road.

We were making our way as a large group of riders to Lake Eildon for lunch. We were travelling at 90 kilometres per hour when we hit the back of their vehicle, and for us our ride finished 20 kilometres before the township of Yea. Sergio was thrown clear of the bike and I apparently slid along the bitumen underneath the Harley, protecting the paintwork!

Once we knew for ourselves that both had survived the crash we were silently and jointly elated, however, neither of us would be walking unaided or be together in close proximity for quite a long time.

In due course an ambulance and the police arrived. I'm not sure if their sirens accompanied them, that much I do not recall. By this stage, many helpful random motorists had also joined us, as had the remaining four Harley bike riders from our original convoy. All of the earlier HOG riders had no idea what had unfolded behind them, although I'm sure this would have become more obvious when they arrived at our pre-designated lunch spot with five unaccounted for motorbikes and their riders.

Once the very heavy motorbike was lifted from on top of me, I was acutely aware of a few things all at once. First, there was petrol leaking out of the tank and onto me; second, the wife of one of the other riders was trying to offer me a cigarette in an unsuccessful attempt to take my mind away from the fact that my left femur was somehow protruding through my brand new Lee jeans at a hideous angle, and for a good ten centimetres. Third, I was keenly aware that the farmer's wife was now kneeling beside me trying to grab my exposed femur with her bare hands, as she uttered, 'What's this?'

Obviously, she was also in shock and totally unaware of the untold infection and possible damage she would have caused to my already very maligned leg bone had she touched it.

With the arrival of the road ambulance I was thankfully able to receive some extremely powerful drugs while still lying on the roadside. My left femur was pushed back inside my ruined leg by the amazing ambulance officers. Because of the severe nature of my injuries a faster form of transport was called for, and I was eventually whisked away in a police helicopter to Melbourne for emergency surgery at the Road Trauma Unit at the Alfred Hospital. The risk of losing my leg was apparently great, as I had already lost a lot of blood and the femur bone was broken in two places. Parts of it were also missing, presumably somewhere on the bitumen.

Compound fractures are never good and this was no exception. It's just not what you ever expect to have happen to you. Apparently, all of this roadside havoc fell under the jurisdiction of the Traffic Accident Commission (TAC), and as a result Sergio was first taken for treatment at the small local bush nursing hospital in Yea. After an initial examination there, an X-ray detected the need for surgery to his ankle. He was then eventually driven by ambulance to the nearest public hospital to the accident site, as per TAC's criteria, which was about 100 kilometres away in the outer northern Melbourne suburb of Maroondah. He was nursing a cracked pelvis, broken lower leg and smashed ankle.

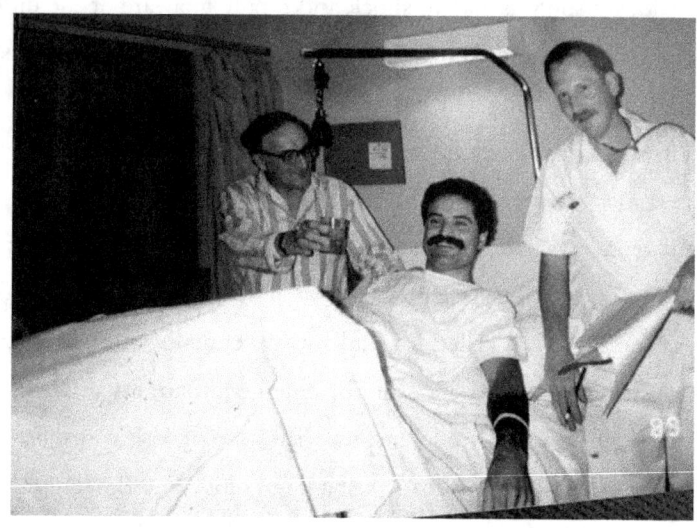

Sergio recovering after Harley crash in 1989

At least we were both quite systematic with our injuries, all of them being kept to the left-hand side of our bodies and not all over, which had been a very real possibility.

After my speedy helicopter flight back to Melbourne, I arrived on the grassy turf of Fawkner Park opposite the Alfred. Sadly, the newly built rooftop helipad was only days away from completion, and I felt every single tiny bump as the ambulance made the very short journey across the lawn to the emergency ward of the Road Trauma Unit. It was here that I had to concede defeat, and completely gave up any hope of ever salvaging my new Lee jeans and having the tear in the front repaired. I had to be cut out of them on both sides in order to be hastily gowned up and taken to one of the emergency surgery rooms. Funny the ridiculous things that you remember in times of great duress.

Just prior to the operation to plate and pin my femur together I remember my mum, Joan, and stepdad, Bill, arriving in a very anxious state from Mansfield. At the accident scene I can vividly remember telling the police, amid all of the chaos, the necessary details for contacting my family. It was the strangest thing, because even though I was full of pain-numbing drugs I could recite Mum and Bill's phone number, relationship to me, names, address and any other information that was required. I can even remember telling them that Bill was a retired policeman, not that this had any bearing at all on the current situation. The weird thing is that sometimes in moments of complete lucidness I can completely forget Mum's phone number, and I often doubt myself that I have their post office box and postcode right when I mail them birthday cards. The mind is an amazing thing and I can never hope to explain for a second how it all works.

My time at the Alfred was quite surreal in so many ways and I can honestly say that it was not all bad in any way. The first operation was my longest and it apparently took over six hours to perform the surgery, which included a bone graft taken from my left hip to fill the missing bits of bone that were forever lost. There was also a long metal plate with sixteen bolts of varying lengths screwed firmly into my left femur, and many stitches to repair the wounds to my lower leg, foot and ankle.

There was also a rather large hole in the front of my leg through which the femur bone had protruded, and this had to be pulled together and stitched closed. It was decided to perform that operation a few days later. My foot had broken bones, but they apparently need to heal on their own so were left untouched.

Every day I had so many friends and family come past to say hello, which was wonderful. On one particular day, a huge, unknown and somewhat sheepish man filled my doorway and asked if I was Kerry. When I answered 'yes', he looked even more surprised. Here I was sitting up in my hospital bed attached to the constant passive movement (CPM) machine, wearing the new powder blue nightie with matching negligee that Mum had just bought for me.

I was sporting a fashionably bright-coloured scrunchie worn on my pony tail and was also wearing a full face of make-up, because I technically wasn't sick – just somewhat incapacitated. Clearly I was not what he was expecting! Sadly I can no longer remember his name, but I invited this very real-looking biker in. He explained he was a volunteer from a group that supported bikers who had encountered motorcycle accidents of any kind, and he had been made aware of our plight. This was all very new to me, and as I was going nowhere fast I could hardly refuse his visit.

In order to establish the facts of the accident and what had transpired beforehand, he was asking me what, if anything, I might have 'taken' or 'smoked' before the accident. Apparently some accidents are not quite as innocent as ours, when determining what's in your system at the time of impact, and the police may have further questions to ask of you! We laughed and laughed when I told him I had smoked an Alpine Light cigarette and drank a skinny cappuccino about thirty minutes before the crash. Nothing hardcore about us and our crash, just bad luck to have it happen and good fortune to have survived it.

I was also amazed that this unknown support group also offers to help cover your rent if needed and care for any pets that may be at home while you are in hospital. I was astounded by the kindness and generosity of this big and burly biker. The nurses gently teased me about my dubious-looking visitor, who came to see me a few times over my month-long stay. I felt extremely grateful that people like this existed in our world.

An unexpected but timely marriage proposal came via telephone from Sergio's ward at Maroondah Base Hospital to my room at the Alfred. I was elated and accepted without hesitation, as I always knew we were very much meant to be together and this cemented our wish to become a fully fledged couple.

Me celebrating our engagement at the Alfred after our motorbike crash

My doctors and nurses were all absolutely brilliant, and after the nurses heard of Sergio's proposal they arranged a lovely cake and bottle of bubbly for me to share with them to celebrate our engagement. On reflection, I'm not so sure that sparkling wine and morphine were such a good mix, but thankfully I had sides on my bed and was not likely to fall out. My lovely physiotherapist even put her own engagement ring on my finger for the day, so I could feel very much 'engaged'.

Finally, a few weeks later Sergio was discharged from hospital and came to see me. He was sitting up in a wheelchair and being pushed by his brother, Robert. A passionate kiss was hard to muster, as I was still attached for twenty hours a day to the CPM machine. Sergio could not stand to reach me and I had lots of difficulty trying to reach far enough downward for our lips to touch. It seems hilarious on reflection, just as it probably was for Robert, who was witnessing our awkward reunion.

Both of us had a variety of metal plates and pins inserted to hold our limbs in place. A huge plate with sixteen screws ran almost from my hip to my knee, holding my femur together, and a rather long screw was keeping Sergio's ankle attached. His cracked hip and broken leg were left to heal in their own time, as was my broken foot and deep lesions on my calf area and left foot. There was altogether a tally of eight operations between us to repair the damage from the motorbike accident, but we did make it through to the other side of good health eventually.

A strange thing happened as soon as we were both discharged from our respective hospitals. Prior to the accident, we both had our own places to call home and lived quite happily in separate locations, but we felt an incredible want and need to never be separated again. One of the consultants at the office told Sergio about a house for sale near to where he lived, in the suburb of Flemington. This appealed greatly, as we really liked this inner city area with its charming old homes and the tree-lined streets.

Both of us had so much difficulty initially in even looking at the house, as it had a few front steps and neither of us was great at mastering crutches and stairs at the same time. The poor real estate agent looked as if we were playing a ridiculous joke on him, and it appeared rather obvious to us that he was desperate for the viewing to be over. I'm sure it took him a while to recover when we called him and made a legitimate offer later that night to buy the house. We were thrilled to purchase our first home together in Finsbury Street, Flemington the week before Christmas and unbelievably just six weeks after the accident.

Joan, Bill and Kiah

It was a short financial settlement, which was perfect for us as we couldn't wait to start our lives together living permanently under the one roof. My wonderful mum and stepdad, Bill, had already very kindly packed up my rented unit in Brunswick West, handed the keys back to the agent and taken my two, no doubt perturbed, cats Slate and Woolley back to enjoy the country life in Mansfield until I was well enough to care for them again.

It was wisely decided by Sergio's family that I should move into the family home in Avondale Heights, to be cared for by Sergio's sister Diana, stepmother Beth and his dad Sam until we were both well enough to make the move into Finsbury Street. It was an extremely kind offer from Sergio's family, and of course I was most welcome to rest and mend with Mum and Bill and my cats in Mansfield, but I just wanted to stay close to Sergio in Melbourne. Two single beds were moved downstairs into the lounge room for both Sergio and me, as there was a toilet downstairs and we definitely could not master climbing a full staircase of stairs each night. Where we bathed is a forgotten mystery to me; presumably we had self-administered sponge baths, but I honestly can't remember. Diana was always exceptionally kind and caring and drove us everywhere we needed to go, and we were most grateful for her generosity.

In late January Finsbury Street officially became ours, and we moved in with the help of family after transporting all of my furnishings and belongings from the rented storage unit nearby in North Melbourne. Sergio had previously shared a house with his brother, Robert, in Kensington and he only had to move in his bed, wardrobe and clothing, which was relatively easy by comparison to my huge haul of collectables!

Once we were deemed fit and well enough to commence physiotherapy, a nearby therapist was found that fell under TAC's jurisdiction in North Melbourne and our twice daily visits commenced in earnest with Maria. By this stage Sergio was driving. I'm actually not sure that this was either wise or legal, but it was what we did in an effort to feel somewhat independent at last. We hated having to rely on Diana or others all the time to get us everywhere, and I'm sure we looked quite novel, both clambering out of the car on wooden crutches on arrival.

Hydrotherapy also commenced as part of our rehabilitation, but only once all of our open wounds had fully healed. All in all, we were slowly becoming more mobile and this was a great feeling at last.

Our newfound state of independence came crashing down one night when Sergio arrived home with a take-away pizza from our favourite shop in Brunswick Street, Fitzroy. The staff had kindly brought it out to the car after Sergio rang them on his then ultra-modern car phone, to alert the shop of his arrival. All good so far, but we soon realised that it is absolutely impossible to carry a pizza upright in a box while on crutches. We quite simply could not get our much anticipated dinner into the house!

A random local was spotted innocently walking past, so Sergio called out to him for assistance. It was the funniest scenario, with Sergio standing by the car on his crutches, the pizza box on the roof and me looking on hopefully from the verandah on my matching walking aids. The poor man gazed from Sergio to the pizza box, to me and back again, looking slightly doubtful about this would-be prank.

He obviously thought the better of it and literally raced past me with our dinner, depositing it hastily on the kitchen bench and then practically running out of the house. Dinner was served, and I bet this unknown neighbour has also dined out on this dinner story for many years.

Finally, I was able to return to work at Franchise Developments in April, about six months after the bike crash. I was still on crutches but also driving my car, the legalities of which are even now unknown to me. Thankfully there was a lift in our building and I had a car park underneath. It was important to try to get back to living a normal life, but it was also rather challenging at times.

A wedding date, subsequent morning ceremony and a lunch had been originally set for some time in June at Roselyn Court in Essendon, a beautiful old Victorian mansion with a rear garden for our outdoor marriage service. However, it was clearly apparent that my leg was not healing as it should have been, and further X-rays showed that the original bone graft had not worked properly. It was back to hospital for more surgery. A new donor site was located at the top of my left hip, above my buttock, and I went through this hellish operation all over again.

July was chosen as our new wedding date. It was extremely advantageous that we opted for a lunch-time wedding, which was not the norm in the nineties, because had we booked a Saturday evening dinner originally there would have been no hope of changing the dates at such short notice. Sometimes breaking the trend has its own rewards! July soon also became out of the question, as although my last lot of surgery was thankfully successful I was still on crutches, and I refused to get married looking so utterly incapacitated.

We were eventually married on 11 August 1990. I got around with the aid of a walking stick, which I wrapped in cream ribbon to match my Mariana Hardwick wedding gown that my dear friend, Jen, had chosen with me on our one and only day of wedding dress shopping. Sergio was able-bodied by this stage, having recovered from the unanticipated diagnosis of superficial gangrene and an ensuing skin graft. His bones had mended, but with all things considered we were both a picture of somewhat dubious-looking good health.

After our wedding night at the lovely old Windsor Hotel in Spring Street, Thailand was our honeymoon destination of choice. We stayed for a few nights at the Montien Hotel, near the Patpong Markets in Bangkok, and then flew to Phuket to fully relax at the Le Meridien Resort for ten nights. Sadly, Sergio had to deal with a horrible bout of severe food poisoning – a bad prawn will do that to you – and he also had a very near miss when a massive bolt of lightning struck the car door just as he stepped into the vehicle.

It was so lucky that he was not still standing in gushing water at that very instant, as the outcome would have been very different indeed. Someone had clearly been watching over and protecting us both. Yes, we had experienced many near misses, but we were both destined to fulfil the most wonderful of roles possible. We just weren't aware of it as yet.

***

It was in Thailand that our daughter, Carla, was conceived, presumably between the food poisoning ordeal and Sergio's near miss with the lightning strike. Our family of two became three just nine months and ten days after marrying, and we could not have been happier. We had always hoped to start a family straight away and we certainly ticked all the boxes right there. I stayed on working at Franchise Developments until Easter the next year, then began to prepare a beautiful nursery for our baby's homecoming. Neither of us wanted to know the sex of the baby; we preferred the old-fashioned way of having a complete surprise on arrival day.

Sergio and I attended pre-natal classes, arranged through the Mercy Maternity Hospital, and we tried to prepare as much as possible with becoming first-time parents. In reality, we were both totally clueless to the ways of babies and any youngsters in general aged under ten.

We followed all of the handy tips given to us at these pre-natal classes, and our bed was 'suited up' with a massive plastic underlay to contain the flow of any unwanted amniotic fluid. I will never forget that when I did actually go into labour my waters broke, resembling the sound of a very loud rubber band snapping, and I was extremely grateful for the foresight of the improvised mattress protector. In his excitement, Sergio accidentally and naively let me know that he was thrilled this drama occurred in our bed and not in our new car on the way to the hospital!

To make matters worse, as I was phoning the hospital to let them know of our baby's impending arrival Sergio was having a shower, so he could arrive clean and fresh to witness the arrival of our first born. I arrived unshowered and unwashed, just desperate to bring this beautiful life that grew within me into the world.

My labour was relatively easy for my first baby, and four and a bit hours later our gorgeous daughter, Carla Maree, arrived into this world weighing 3.2 kilograms, sporting short and very dark hair like her dad. My pregnancy had been a dream: no morning sickness or back pain, my dicky left leg staying intact and presenting no real trouble. Carla was the most beautiful and easy of babies imaginable when she entered this world on Tuesday, 21 May 1991.

The first year of married life started out in our new home in Finsbury Street, Flemington, where Carla and I had a wonderful time getting to know one another. I had barely held a baby before Carla's birth, let alone cared for one, and yet it came so easily to me. It was all instinctive and it felt so utterly right.

We started attending a small new mother's group that consisted of six first-time mums and their babes at the Infant Welfare Centre in Kensington. It was here, aged just three weeks, that Carla met her first real friend, a beautiful little bub called Carly whose mum just happened to be also called Kerrie.

It was a funny coincidence with the names, as we all just gelled and still do twenty-six years later. It's always interesting, I think, how certain people come into your life at certain times. Some are there for brief encounters and others for the long haul.

When Carla was one year old, a perfect and much sought-after landmark home went on the market in Farnham Street, only three streets away from where we were living. We had often walked past this large and interesting-looking house, always admiring it and often wondering what lay within.

After a couple of inspections with various real estate agents and very little negotiation on my part, as Sergio was away on business in Adelaide, I felt like a woman possessed who simply had to buy this house. Prior to his trip, Sergio had given me a financial limit to keep in the back of my mind during the haggling process, but in the excitement of the impending transaction I threw caution to the wind and went straight to my optimum figure. Our dream home became a reality. We were able to buy this wonderful old Victorian charmer prior to the scheduled auction in June 1992.

The house had 'good bones', as they say, but it also needed a very large, long and expensive renovation to bring it back to its former glory. Unlike most families, who tend to move out when they renovate, we chose to move in, and somehow it all seemed perfectly normal to be having and raising babies while living through a major house restoration. We all took it in our stride.

We were absolutely thrilled to learn that we had another baby on the way but, unlike with Carla, my pregnancy was not as smooth as hoped. I rebroke my already extremely fragile femur by stepping not so carefully off the verandah and landing on my damaged left leg instead of my good right one. The very long plate and sixteen screws had been removed the year before and my honeycomb-looking femur was very weak, to say the least, and it could not cope with me accidentally landing on the wrong leg. Too late, the damage was done: I had a spiral fracture straight through the middle of my femur that thankfully stayed intact and together as I limped around on it in total denial for ten days!

It was back to my orthopaedic surgeon, David Young, for X-rays (with a huge lead apron placed over my tummy to protect our unborn baby) and the horrible prognosis was confirmed. The only positive thing about breaking your leg midway through a pregnancy is that apparently your body is humming with all sorts of healing hormones that will hasten the mending of the bones. Thank you for small mercies and strange miracles.

The remaining three and a half months of my pregnancy were spent back on crutches, while also wearing a massive protective brace on my upper left leg. Another glitch occurred only weeks before the baby was about to make its grand entrance into the world: it had decided to arrive feet first as an undiagnosed breach birth, which is neither great for the baby nor the mother.

Without going into the gory specifics, the baby was delivered very hastily, thanks to a random doctor who just happened to be standing outside my delivery room door at the Mercy Hospital. My obstetrician had been telephoned too late, and by then our beautiful son had already emerged, ankles first. Samuel James was born on Saturday, 13 March 1993. Welcome to the world, baby Sam!!

**

Our family of four settled down remarkably easily to home life at Farnham Street. We were extremely fortunate that I was able to stay at home to care for both Carla and Sam throughout their early childhood, and also into the later years when both attended Flemington Primary School just up the road. Our days were full and fun and we made many firm friends, first at St Brendan's Kindergarten, where both Carla and Sam attended, and then more wonderful friendships at primary school.

Ours was a family like so many others, nothing visibly different or special: mum, dad, daughter, son and two new cats, Jingles and Megan, who had replaced lovely old Woolley and Slate, who by this stage had both gone to God. We lived a life that was full and rich in the poetic sense of the word, with Carla and Sam enjoying tennis and swimming lessons, drama classes, dancing for Carla, Auskick and Vic Cric for Sam, birthday parties, local footy training and Saturday school sport with Wesley College.

Jingles and Megan

When Carla and Sam were younger we had a lot of regular trips and holidays to various places, some near home and others interstate. New Zealand was our first overseas trip of choice as a family, mainly because it was short in travel time, culturally not too different, and it just seemed like the perfect starting point.

Travel became a big part of our lives, and I firmly believe that our trips away together as a family strengthened our already strong bond and further enriched our connection with each other. We loved being immersed in all sorts of new cultures, and when travelling together you also learn many new things about your own family dynamics that are not always so apparent when at home.

From a very early age Sam had always been a thoroughly entertaining boy, and when on family holidays he somehow took his comedic performances to new levels of hilarity. We all loved Sam's antics and the private shows he put on in our hotel room after a great day out.

We never knew what Sam had planned in the way of entertainment; he would choreograph his moves in private and just let loose. Once in Hanoi, Vietnam, Sam was found by Carla in our wardrobe wearing the hotel's white towelling bathrobe while it was still on the hanger attached to the rack. It made him look like a modern-day Quasimodo, but with no neck.

He was in there hiding and laying in wait, knowing that Carla would discover him sooner or later, and when she did they were hysterically laughing and rolling around on the floor. Sam would take it upon himself to conjure up funny new ideas and tricks for each and every holiday, and away he would go and get the show started.

On another occasion, we had barely arrived in Narita, Japan, when Sam put on a one-man show. He was dressed this time in the hotel kimono with the sash belt tied around his head, like the Karate Kid, while busting some martial art moves between the beds. Sam was a born entertainer; he aimed to please, impress and leave his mark upon you, and he most certainly succeeded in touching us all in the most remarkable ways.

It was not necessarily intentional, but we were the 'party house'. There's always one, and we were it. Ours was a home where all were welcome and both generations loved having gatherings by the pool, barbeques, parties, drinks at the kitchen bench and meals around the large dining tables, both inside and out. I didn't realise at the time how important these stabilising years were for all of us. It was here that great and lasting friendship foundations were laid and built upon, not just for Sergio and me but for Carla and Sam, too.

 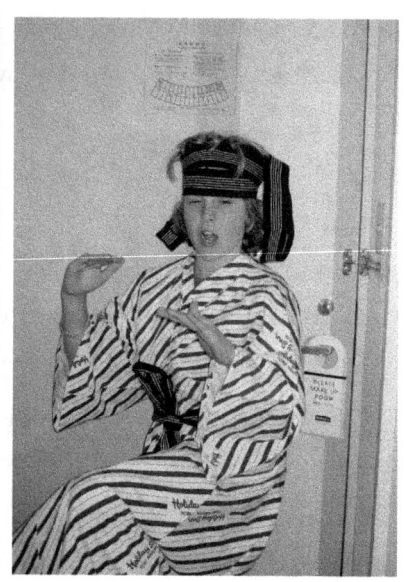

Quasimodo in Vietnam *Karate Kid in Japan*

CHAPTER 2

About Sam

Sam was always different to other boys in so many ways. By different, I mean that there was a uniqueness about him that didn't seem readily apparent in other boys of his young years. From a very early age Sam had an exceptionally caring and nurturing side to him. He worried about how you felt, what you thought and how you were coping in certain situations.

When Sam started his extra long kinder stint at St Brendan's Kindergarten, he was so excited to have his turn there. Carla had been attending this wonderful kinder for a year already, and Sam was very aware of our routine of dropping her off and seeing all the other little kids and witnessing first hand all the fun they were having. Sam was so keen to join in this organised mayhem that I asked Mrs O'Dwyer, the principal, if Sam could start his early childhood tuition the next year and do two years of three-year-old kinder instead of the normal one year and then the following year in four-year-old kinder.

Sam was intentionally held back by us from starting primary school too early, as he was a March baby and we didn't want him starting school too young. We worried about how this may affect his latter years of secondary school. I look back now and wonder why we all worry so much about such things, that in the greater scheme of things mean so very little indeed, but I was not privy to this knowledge at the time.

Sam and kinder got along just fine and he absolutely loved going for his couple of two-hourly sessions per week. We still had Carla doing four-year-old kinder, so I would do the quick trip to St Brendan's at lunch time to bring her home, hastily feed them both, and then race back to deliver Sam for his short stint in the afternoon.

Both Carla and Sam were children who constantly displayed a lot of open affection to us, and to all they loved. It always made Miss Rosemary, the assistant, and Mrs O'Dywer laugh when Sam would kiss the entire length of my arm each time I left after dropping him off. He did it with so much gusto and love, a real sense of fun and always with genuine affection. It tended to resemble Gomez Addams kissing Morticia on *The Addams Family*!

As a youngster at kindergarten, Sam was the only boy continually being invited to the numerous fairy parties that seemed to be held every other weekend. Although Carla could encourage him to wear fairy wings and tutus at home, this simply would not do outside of our walls. A wizard cape with evil eyes at the back was purchased from a local fete, and Sam happily went off to all the girls' parties clutching his gift and with his cape trailing behind him.

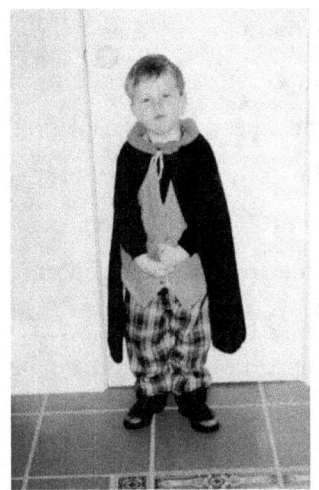
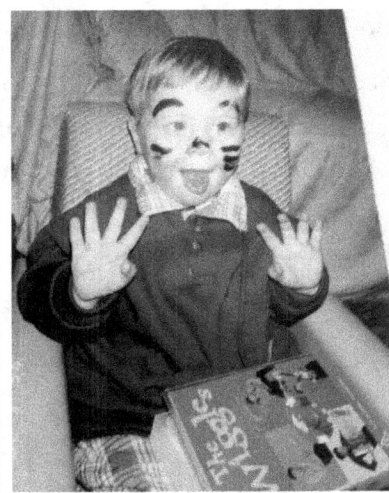

Sam in his wizard cape and in party mode

Carla and Sam were both a joy to be with. Sergio and I really did have an amazing time watching them play, engaging with them and taking them out to wherever we needed to go. We quite simply just loved sharing our lives all together. Growing up, Sam would play any games that Carla dreamt up for them both, and playing grocery shops for hours on end was always a joint favourite. However, I noticed that Sam rarely ever seemed to be the cashier, always just the customer, but this never seemed to bother him. He was with Carla, whom he totally adored, and that was all that really mattered.

I distinctly remember Sam and I visiting Sergio at the John Fawkner Hospital in Coburg after he had cracked his hip in a cycling accident (one of many over the years). Carla was away from home for the week on a school camp with Wesley College, and we had not broken the bad news to her at that stage about her dad's latest cycling injury.

While waiting for the doctors to finish seeing Sergio on their routine visit, Sam and I went to have a snack and coffee at the hospital's cafeteria. Sam immediately noticed that the young girl behind the counter was in training, as her badge told us so. I'm not sure how many other eleven-year-old boys would even register this, let alone compute that she would be feeling nervous and unsure in her new job role.

Sam asked that I be gentle with her when being served. I'm still not sure what type of outburst he was expecting from his mum, but gentle I was. To this day, I am both inwardly and outwardly so very proud of our boy for recognising the needs of a complete stranger. This incredibly sensitive and nurturing side of Sam was always so very apparent to us and to his many, many friends. As we chatted about her, Sam said it was important to give everyone new to a job encouragement and support, especially in their early days, so as not to break their spirit! Hats off to you my son, quite impressive indeed.

Sam made friends very easily, judged no one and would often include the kids on the perimeter in his fold. Sporty and musical, Sam enjoyed his footy, tennis, cricket and swimming in his younger years and preferred to be more of a spectator in these areas as he matured. Trumpet and guitar lessons were replaced by a love of music, both live and recorded, and his musical tastes were as varied as his friendships. New connections were made and old ones kept, as Sam started secondary school at Wesley College in St Kilda Road, where Carla was already a student. Social activities overtook academic endeavours and Sam's circle of friends grew exponentially.

Clockwise from left: Sam A. and Sam O.; Sam after a footy game at Moonee Valley; me and Sam at graduation from Flemington Primary School

Our annual trips overseas continued, and Sam was forever buying soccer tops for his friends back home and also many pairs of mildly offensive boxer shorts from the markets in Florence that focused on the crotch region of Michelangelo's David! Typical of Sam, he just wanted everyone to have a laugh and benefit from our travels and to share something fun with others. He was forever thoughtful of everyone, and this did not go unnoticed by us or by his extended family and friends.

We reciprocated the many birthday party invitations over the years by having parties at our home or at the local Flemington neighbourhood house over the road. Here, the footy could be kicked and the kids could run riot in the park. In Sam's younger years, the predominantly all-boy invitees would feast on his favourite party cuisine, 'freezer food', as he called it, which consisted of party pies, hot chips, pizza, chicken nuggets and small hot dogs. These parties were noisy, boisterous, wet, testosterone laden and loads of fun. On reflection, the same menu still applied in the later years, only then we added girls and alcohol to the mix!

The birthday gatherings continued, both at our house and at a host of other locations. Sam never needed an excuse to celebrate anything; our boy always loved to party. Girls other than Carla and her friends also started to appear on the scene, and these celebrations took on another dimension. The girls all seemed to love Sam, and from what we could gather he loved them back.

Sam and Carla with Nan and Pop

Family was always first and foremost for Sam and Carla alike. It is a wonderful way to be, and I have always admired them both for having these very special qualities. Grandparents, aunts, uncles and cousins were always a high priority and family events were never a chore but rather something to look forward to, whether it be a trip on the bus or in the car to Nan and Pop's in Mansfield for a few days, or just visiting their Nonno for a bowl of pasta.

As the last years of high school were reached, Sergio and I decided that our much-loved annual family trips away could not happen because of the need to study for exams. We both understood the reasoning behind this completely, but I felt that half of us could still go away for a special one-on-one experience. When Carla was doing her VCE year Sam and I flew off for two and a half fantastic weeks together in the USA, going to Disneyland in Anaheim, Las Vegas, New York and San Francisco.

Initially, Sam was a tiny bit sceptical about just he and I heading off together, but Carla's endorsement of 'Mum's actually quite cool, Sam' did the trick, and he felt that I was worth a chance. I had recently had a dream trip to France for four weeks with Carla, her best friend Anna, and her mum, Chris. Apparently, I had excelled in the eyes of my daughter and passed all of the rigorous tests to be deemed 'cool'! Well done to Chris and me, having also passed according to Anna.

My holiday away with Sam was absolutely fantastic on every level. We had the time of our lives together, sharing all of these wonderful experiences in a new country that we had not previously explored. I'm really not sure how many other sixteen-year-old boys would love pool time with their mum, but that's what we did to reinvigorate ourselves as soon as we arrived, slightly jetlagged in Anaheim. Sam had found an inflatable beach ball and a lengthy game of 'catchy' commenced.

The joys of Disneyland were next, and luckily for Sam I am a woman who has never grown up when it comes to fast rides and corny adventures. I am up for it all, and we had so much fun for two days and a night, riding, screaming and soaring our way through both adjacent theme parks. Universal Studios was also on our radar, and that completed day three in the US of A. Brilliant fun and the best of memories for us both. Mine still linger strongly, and I know that Sam's were always held so dearly.

We fully embraced the wackiness of Las Vegas, even though Sam was a minor and I am a non-gambler. For us, our three nights at the Bellagio hotel were amazing. We went to see a different show after dinner each night, Cirque du Soleil's *O*, *The Lion King* and the Blue Man Group, playing at the Venetian, at Sam's suggestion.

We rode the crazy roller coaster at New York, New York that departs from right inside the hotel: off you go, swirling, swivelling and hyperventilating into the desert sun. Certainly not for everyone, but for Sam and me it was bliss. It was perfect, and it was just us. To top things off we took a helicopter ride and champagne breakfast (for Mum) at the base of the Grand Canyon, a very surreal way to start any day and one that you cannot possibly ever forget.

New York beckoned for the next week and we could not resist its charms. I had heard so many wonderful things from Sergio and others about this iconic city, and it certainly did not disappoint. We stayed on Broadway in the Upper West, not far from Central Park, which was where we ended up most days. We rode bikes, walked, ate ice creams, and Sam simply had to experience the obligatory hot dog stands!

Sam at the Grand Canyon

Galleries and museums were not Sam's strengths, and I was blissfully aware of this. I did, however, manage to encourage a short two-hour visit to the Frick gallery, in exchange for four plus hours exploring Ripley's Believe It or Not. A fair trade, and we both had a fantastic day.

We also included a bit of culture into our stay, and the memory of our tour into Harlem to attend a gospel church service and hear the choir sing stays with me to this day. It was so moving, humbling and amazing, and Sam absolutely loved the experience as well. You don't need to have any understanding of religion or the beliefs of the congregation in these churches to fully appreciate the raw passion and emotion for all that they honour, trust and believe in. Sam had barely entered a church in his short lifetime, and I am so happy that I was able to give him this amazing experience of hearing a gospel service that relied on the magic of music and was not weighed heavily with words that often mean not so much.

I remember arriving in San Francisco and making a dash for the bathroom, leaving Sam to collect our cases from the baggage carousel. When I returned, here he was helping an elderly lady with her luggage and getting it all sorted for her. She asked if he was my son, and I proudly answered 'yes'. I felt so pleased that such a small gesture on Sam's part could mean so much to a total stranger. Sam always knew where to step in and help; he certainly didn't require me there to direct him. Well done, my love.

San Francisco was our final stop. I chose this city because it sounded exciting and different, but in reality I truly didn't care where we were. We were together having a ball and that was all that really mattered. We spent many hours down at Pier 39 at Fisherman's Wharf watching the antics of the sea lions, as they swam in from the wild and beached themselves on the specially built heavy duty pontoons. They were hilarious with their shenanigans, all the males trying to rule each tiny 'island' and not allow other males to climb on board. It was totally enjoyable to see, and the seafood chowder eaten later on at the restaurant on the pier was not too bad either.

Our hotel was very central, just down from Union Square. One morning Sam handed me a brochure he had picked up at reception, about an architectural walking tour to look at Victorian houses in the Pacific Heights area. How special was that? I loved a nice walk and anything to do with grand old homes always had my attention. We joined the tour and Sam was clearly the youngest by at least thirty years, but this did not bother him at all. He chose this outing for me and for my passions; it was his way of giving back for the wonderful trip we were having. It was not necessary, but so very much appreciated.

It seemed silly to visit San Francisco and not see Alcatraz Island, so a ferry across was booked on the recommendation of our travel agent months prior to leaving Melbourne. This way we had a pre-determined leaving time, but it was up to us when we made the return journey back.

Sam and I stepped off our ferry, after spending a few amazing hours learning all about the horrors of Alcatraz prison and its inmates. It was then that I heard the name 'Da Vinci' being called, a nickname given to Sam while at Wesley College. What are the chances? I turned to see Sam and two other boys in a full and affectionate embrace. I also noticed one of the boys' mums, whom I happened to know vaguely, standing beside me. It was surreal: here we were with some of Sam's Wesley mates on the other side of the world, randomly bumping into each other. A dinner date was promptly made for that night, our last one in the USA as it turned out.

Noah, Sam and Alex in San Francisco

Dinner was held in a private dining room at Slanted Door, a fantastic modern Vietnamese restaurant in the old ferry terminal. Sam and I were the first to arrive, and I couldn't help but notice that our dining table had bunches of Australian wattle in vases along the whole length of the table. How very appropriate, given that we were three Australian families. We all had the most fantastic night; it heralded the end of our very special mum and son trip. I know that Noah and Alex both shared amazing memories with their respective families as well.

We flew home the next night feeling absolutely exhausted after a day of walking everywhere and cramming in as many last-minute things as possible. When our flight left at midnight, we both rested our heads together supporting one another, Sam to my right and me to his left. We drifted off to sleep before we even left the tarmac and stayed like this for about six hours. I'm sure that the flight staff smiled at this picture of a sleeping mum and her son, with a little bit of happy emotion in their own hearts.

All through our holiday Sam and I shared a room and so much more. It is these beautiful memories that I hold so very dear to my heart, now and forever more. We were meant to take that trip away together, just us two. It was our time, our special moment in life, and I am so glad I listened to the voice within telling me as much.

* * *

During Sam's final year at Wesley College, when he was studying his VCE, I decided to book a fantastic-looking house at Apollo Bay, on the coast, during the September school holiday break, so that Sam could immerse himself in his studies and prepare properly for the upcoming exams in October and November. Sergio had done a similar thing with Carla when she was doing her VCE two years earlier, and they had a very productive and enjoyable week staying at Bright, in Victoria's high country.

Literally on the day Sam and I were leaving for Apollo Bay we both noticed that Jingles, Sam's ginger tabby cat, had sunk into a bit of a depressed state, as she sometimes did when her systematic routine was upset in any way. She instinctively knew we were up to something that did not include her. She had seen the bags being packed, she was no fool, this meant desertion on our part!

Sam with Jingles

Neither of us wanted to leave her for the week, even though Carla and Sergio were still at home, so we made a quick decision to take Jingles with us on her first-ever holiday. A trip to the local supermarket was made for another kitty litter tray and a bag of litter, her food for the week and a nice new little flannel blanket, and Jingles was all packed and ready to go. Megan, Carla's cat, stayed home, which was probably preferable, as these two finicky felines had no time for one another (and still don't) and there was no love lost in removing Jingles for a week.

We left a note for Sergio and Carla to explain Jingles' absence and off we set, with me driving the three-hour road trip to Apollo Bay. Jingles stayed firmly on Sam's lap, sitting on her new paw print blanket for the duration of the drive, and Sam proceeded to work his way through his pre-planned playlist of music.

Thanks to Sam I now love Eminem. He first introduced me to Eminem's music when the movie *Eight Mile* hit our movie screens in 2003. At the time I was not aware of the content of the movie, the story line or anything to do with Eminem, and I wondered why I was getting so many very dark and strange looks from the other movie patrons as I took my ten-year-son to see this film. As it turned out, it was not age appropriate in any way, shape or form for Sam but the damage was done. We were there in the dark enjoying Eminem's life story and his music. Sam knew exactly what he was doing even if I didn't, and I'm sure he scored a few points with his primary school mates after this interesting movie outing with his mum!

Bliss n Eso were also on Sam's playlist, not so much to my taste but I really didn't care – we were heading away to the beach together for a week, with the added bonus of having Jingles with us, and it was all absolutely fantastic. The house was as wonderful as we had hoped for. We chose our respective bedrooms, and Jingles freelanced between the two. Sam set a study plan into action, and I have honestly never seen him apply himself so keenly and diligently to his studies. Things were looking up: it was a little late into his secondary school career, but it was happening.

Sergio came to visit and stayed with us for the weekend. We cooked up a big barbeque lunch and watched the AFL footy grand final on TV. Life was good, and very positive in every way. On the Monday, Sam and I packed up our belongings, left the house totally intact and located Jingles, who was hiding under a bed. She sensed that another car trip was imminent and was keen to stay firmly pinned to the carpet by all four paws.

The October tests and end of year exams came and went and Sam's study plan and associated hard work paid off. He passed his VCE and was accepted at Victoria University to study criminal justice.

Sam's 18th birthday party

All through secondary school both Carla and Sam had small part-time jobs. Sam's days working at the local Video Ezy were behind him, and he was now working as a waiter at our restaurant, Amigos, on Hardware Lane in the city and also at another Amigos on Lygon Street in Carlton.

With high school now complete, the opportunity arose for Sam to join a small group of friends from Wesley and head off to Thailand for five or six weeks. It was his turn to enjoy time away without his family, instead being in the company of great friends. This was their gap year between high school and university, a chance to work, rest, party and play. There was so very much to look forward to, or so we all thought.

Jeremy and Sam in Thailand, 2012

It has never been lost on me that in the final week of Sam's short but full life, both he and Carla took their three younger cousins, Loren, Maddi and Millie (whom they were minding for the week), to have dinner with their eighty-eight-year-old Nonno, who lived in the suburb of Avondale Heights. They got to have a first and final 'road trip' all together, albeit only a sixteen kilometre journey.

Unfortunately, both Jack and Ruby, their smaller cousins, were not at this last supper, as they were very young at the time. Nevertheless, this one and only evening with five of Nonno's grandchildren did take place, without any of us parents being there. Nonno loved every second of that very special last dinner together, and so did all the kids. In a way, this was the beginning of the signs and pointers of things to unfold, not just in that week but in all the months and years to come.

Family fun at Farnham Street Park

Sam, Nonno and Carla

CHAPTER 3

The accident

On 2 May 2012 I got home from work late, which was quite normal, after hosting at Amigos, the city-based restaurant that we co-own. I went to bed feeling slightly uneasy and tense, not a regular mood for me. It was then that Sam sent me a text close to midnight, saying he would be staying with his mate, Kai, at his place, as more friends, Liv, Tim and Billy had just arrived. It all made total sense for Sam to stay and it was not at all out of the ordinary for this to happen, but something still did not feel right for me. Sam was always a very good communicator and we greatly appreciated that he let us know what his movements would be.

Sleep didn't come easily to me that night. I had the most vivid and worrying of dreams, about the police coming to see me at our restaurant in Hardware Lane and leading me away in tears. I awoke the next day feeling very troubled by the dream and all morning I felt unusually flat and sad.

I put this all down to it being the thirty-fourth anniversary of my wonderful dad's passing in 1978, in a workplace accident. I was only eighteen years old at the time and my darling dad was a mere forty-eight. He gave his life trying to save that of one of his work colleagues, Alastair, who was twenty-six years old and a newly married man. Tragically, neither of them came home that night, and it was the police who came to my workplace at the Shepparton Preserving Company to tell me the horrific news. My life was forever changed, as was my mum's and sister's, and of course that of Alastair's young bride.

Later that morning, as I was walking down to my city-bound tram, I felt this extremely strong urge to call Sam just to say hello and to see how his night with old school friends had gone. I rarely rang Sam in the morning, as he was not an early riser; he and late nights were far better acquainted. We had a lovely chat, and Sam explained he was all organised to pick up his three younger cousins from school later that day to take them back to their home in Moonee Ponds. Dinner was to be his signature pasta dish of Napoli sauce with Italian sausage, and he was looking forward to cooking it for them.

As already mentioned, both Sam and Carla were co-sharing the minding of their younger cousins, Loren, Maddi and Millie, then aged sixteen, fourteen and twelve, while their parents, Robert and Nadine, were having a brief business trip to the USA. Carla was on duty the first night and then Sam took over, the plan being to rotate with each other for the week. It was regarded as a great coup on Sam's part. He was chuffed to be asked to do something that came with so much responsibility, and he took his role as carer very seriously. He loved all of his cousins very much, and in many ways was the big brother all of the girls and his little cousins Jack and Ruby never had.

Sam and I chatted until I arrived at my tram stop on Mount Alexander Road. He farewelled me with 'Catch you later, I love you, Mum'. Simple, reassuring and heartfelt words came easily to Sam. That was it, time to go. I had a tram to catch and he had things to do before he collected the girls in our family car at 3.30 pm that day. It was 11.30 am when we spoke. I did not know that Sam would later drive in the direction of the Northcote train station, presumably to drop off his mates, Raph and Jesse, to go their separate ways.

At approximately 1.30 pm no one went anywhere as expected and all hell broke loose.

It was a wet, wild and windy day in Melbourne, a typical winter's day but not a day with a typical or anticipated ending. My brother-in-law, Robert, called me from Las Vegas to say that the Flemington police had been to our house in Farnham Street looking for us. They took down the registration number from the car parked in our carport and subsequently called him.

Neither Carla nor Sam had wanted to ferry the girls around in Robert and Nadine's large four-wheel drive and chose to drive one of our two cars instead. The police told Robert that our Mercedes had been involved in an earlier accident and they were trying to find the owners of the car. The severity of the accident was not mentioned, and no other information was forthcoming.

When Robert called me he was sounding calm on the surface. He is a lawyer, cool professionally, but I also sensed in him that all was not well. I rang the police station number that Robert gave me and was quickly passed on to another number. They clearly had information that was not about to be readily shared.

When I was asked if the media had already contacted me, I began to feel sick to the pit of my stomach. Still no answers, just more staying on the line, someone was about to talk to me.

I can't remember his name, rank or voice, but I do know that this was certainly not the first time he had made a call of this nature. Yes, there had been a car accident, that much he could confirm. No, he couldn't give any more details over the phone; he needed to see me in person. A hospital visit to see how Sam was recovering seemed to be totally out of the question; no one was even giving me this option. My dream, my premonition, was now a reality about to unfold. I could neither turn it back nor off; it was there, and as real as it could be.

I gave him my location details, and now this seasoned and controlled policeman knew where to find me. I sat outside our restaurant in the cold and rain staring down towards Lonsdale Street, not daring to turn my iPad on to look at the news sites. Phone calls were made to both Sergio and Carla: 'Where are you?', 'What's happening?' Still no answers. None of us had any idea what was really going on.

Eventually they both arrived separately, thankfully each with a close friend who knew our family very well, and we five collectively slumped together outside Amigos in the cold and wet under the protective awning and waited.

Generally when the constabulary is called for you await their arrival with anticipation and gladness, but this was not the case for us. There was the caller, whose name still escapes me. He was large, experienced and exceptionally humane, and had with him a policewoman, which confirmed my worst fears. In the case of a passing, either workplace, car accident or anywhere else, it seems that both sexes are required to deliver the tragic news. It happened that way with my dad's accident, too.

We all shook hands and went to our tequila and tapas bar upstairs. Luke and Peter, who had arrived with Carla and Sergio, waited outside. They no doubt spoke to our staff, to whom I had failed at this stage to mention anything about what was going on. How could I? I had nothing that made any sense at all to tell.

It is said that people somehow step up in times of extreme adversity, and we witnessed this first hand that day. Once those final words were delivered by that large and caring policeman, and hands were held by his equally caring female colleague, it was our beautiful daughter, Carla, who stepped up to the plate and took over on our behalf.

After huge hugs, copious tears and the dropping of the F bomb by me, our young daughter became the one in control of our family. She answered the policeman's questions about who, from a very long list of potential passengers, might have been with Sam at the time of the accident.

There was a further dilemma for the police, and for us, as the car had apparently exploded in the boot region and there was a subsequent fire. No one knew who was actually in the car, as the bodies could not be identified without DNA samples from the parents. This is where Carla truly moved into the role of the adult and took total charge of the situation, and I'm truly not sure what Sergio and I became.

We are forever grateful that Carla took on the seemingly impossible task of calling Sam's mates one by one on her mobile, to see who answered their phones and who didn't. Many of Sam's friends were her mates too, so she had lots of their contact details.

The process of elimination had begun. Those who answered were given an 'It's okay, just seeing if you were with Sam today' and a hasty hang up. Some were getting more than curious; it had been hours since the accident, and vague news reports were apparently already on the TV and radio. Rumours were beginning to spread about who was involved in this well-publicised car accident.

Our darling twenty-year-old daughter held her head and her own, as she whittled down the possible candidates for who may have just passed away with her beloved nineteen-year-old brother.

The world stood still; time literally stopped. This could not possibly be happening to our Sam, to me, to Sergio, to Carla, to our family and friends, both Sam's and ours. It felt like things had just kicked up a gear, metaphorically speaking.

Carla continued to make calls and we all silently prayed that the owner of that mobile phone number would answer, thus allowing this hideous game of Russian roulette to continue. It did have to finish somewhere; we all just wanted to prolong the inevitable. Raph's number was dialled, Sam's big, beautiful and quirky mate whom he knew from Wesley College and someone who spent many a night at ours, and Sam at his home. Raph never answered his phone, so we sadly found our first 'missing' passenger.

Sergio somehow found his senses and he too once again became an adult in control, starting to make calls as well. It seemed so confronting, ridiculous and totally not possible or feasible that he was calling Nan and Pop, his siblings and close friends to say that Sam and two friends, as yet not properly identified, had passed away at approximately 1.30 pm on Westgarth Street in Northcote after somehow clipping a parked car and then hitting a tree on the nature strip.

It was impossible to understand, and yet there it was. We did not have two uniformed and very concerned police officers standing in our tequila bar for no reason. I now understood that there would not be a trip to the emergency ward of a nearby city hospital to see Sam, smother him with hugs and kisses and pray for a quick and complete recovery. This was so very clearly not an option that we were being offered.

I remember going to the bathroom upstairs at Amigos with Carla and feeling numb. Neither of us said much; we were both in shock, emotions were in chaos. Neither of us was game to show the other the raw pain and agony of what was slowly becoming apparent. We left the restaurant via our downstairs kitchen and dining area. I felt that I needed to say something to our staff, but I actually have no idea what I said. Sam had worked as a waiter part time at our restaurant since completing his VCE the year before. He was one of them, a mate and work colleague, part of that very team. The ripple effect was only just getting started.

My horrible dream from the night before had become a reality, my premonition had come true. I was led away in tears by the police down Hardware Lane that cold, wet and rainy May afternoon, then back to the Northcote Police Station. Mouth swabs were needed, DNA testing was called for, the ensuing fire after the crash had left the police no choice: they too needed to know for certain who the three car occupants were. All of the police involved were extremely kind, caring and understanding. Many were parents too, and this tragedy touched many more people than just us.

I remember arriving back home to Farnham Street. It was freezing, dark and still wet, and I honestly thought it was about midnight. In reality it was only around 6.30 pm and the grapevine in Flemington and beyond was alive with yet to be confirmed reports of the passing of three young men, one of whom was our Sam. These tragedies seem to have a way of becoming news so very quickly.

Our home immediately started to get busy, with people coming from everywhere and the house phone and mobiles never stopping. We still needed to know who else had been in the car with Sam and Raph.

Among the many friends who arrived to pay their respects was an eighteen-year-old family friend, Giulia, who while at our home received a phone call from her girlfriend Alice. Alice called to say that her boyfriend, Jesse, could not be found and she was worried sick. Jesse and Raph were apparently close mates, after meeting in Year 12 at Swinburne College, where Raph had transferred to and studied the year before.

We had another name, another possible victim, which Carla passed on to the police. Another family gave DNA swabs that night.

CHAPTER 4

The days after

It's actually really hard to properly express what happened over the ensuing days, as each one was full of every possible human emotion, strangely enough including laughter. As our dining room area filled continually with friends, family and the occasional new and unknown face, the house became transformed. Photos of Sam made their way to the dining table, and these seemed to be added to each day. The room became an organic shrine that grew and changed with each new visit, as some friends brought new photos along with them. Every surface had something of or about Sam on it. This was extremely helpful when old friends of ours arrived who had never had the opportunity or pleasure of meeting Sam, for they could either openly or discreetly look around at the photos and get a real sense of who he was, and I hasten to add still 'is'.

The kitchen bench became a servery to whoever was there, and thankfully there were always lots of beautiful people continually popping past. Food, wine and beer also miraculously appeared, and was much appreciated and also very much required by us and everyone else visiting Farnham Street.

Lovely old friends, some we hadn't seen much of over recent years (only because our kids all went their different ways after primary school), also seemed to appear, as if on an unwritten roster, to stand post in the kitchen pouring drinks, making cups of tea and coffee and divvying up the cakes, sandwiches, biscuits, casseroles, pastries, cheeses and fruit that covered the kitchen benchtops. It was truly amazing, and so very much welcomed by all of us.

Flowers also started to appear seemingly from nowhere. We would go to bed at night and open the front door the next morning to find that deliveries had been made while we slept. Not everyone is comfortable with having a face-to-face encounter with a newly bereaved parent or sibling, and I can understand how hard it is to do this. But the heartfelt words in their cards certainly left us in no doubt that we all were loved and never far from their thoughts.

The doorbell rang constantly, as floral delivery drivers brought masses of much appreciated flowers sent in Sam's honour to our home. Our family room became a makeshift florist, filled with amazingly beautiful bouquets, bunches, wreaths and arrangements.

It was here where I first truly started sensing a change in the energy and feel to our home. Each night as it got dark, which was very early on those winter evenings in May, I would go into this lovely old family room that had once been a horse stable, complete with huge double stable doors leading directly out onto the street. It had a massively high pitched timber ceiling with huge wooden beams, and it felt almost like a place of worship. The room felt calm and serene, and it looked simply beautiful and all awash with every imaginable colour and perfume.

For some strange reason, possibly because it was close to most people's dinner hour, we never seemed to have visitors at this time of day, so the room was mine to enjoy alone. Without fail, I instantly felt Sam's very presence among the hundreds of cards and botanical offerings. It was a beautiful feeling, and I just felt so happy to be in that space with those beautiful floral tributes and, dare I say, with Sam.

The night after the accident, Carla in particular felt very compelled to have us three visit where the boys had passed on Westgarth Street, Northcote. I remember really wanting to take something to the accident site to leave in Sam's honour, and after much deliberation I took a framed photograph of the four of us that was taken on our last holiday all together, in Italy in 2010. I also added a glass and silver candle holder complete with candle, from the same trip. It was a pitiful offering, but who the hell knows what to do at these times?

Our family, Como, Italy, 2010

It was both nerve-racking and confronting to arrive at the accident location in the cold and dark of early sunset. We could clearly see the charred ruin of what was once a fully grown tree, and it seemed utterly surreal to think that Sam, Raph and Jesse had lost their lives at this very spot only yesterday.

There were young friends everywhere keeping vigil, burning candles, leaving letters, keepsakes and private offerings. I will never forget how, when the three of us were recognised, everyone sitting all stood up and formed an impromptu guard of honour that parted the sea of grief, allowing us to come forward with our meagre offering. Jesse's long-term girlfriend, Alice, came to us and introduced herself. We all hugged, and there were more tears all round. The grief and love surrounding the location was almost tangible.

The sheer number of letters, tributes and messages left at the crash site for all of the three boys was both amazing and totally overwhelming. It was in this very place of total sadness and loss that another small miracle occurred, and three friends of mine all had a part to play.

An old workmate, Bron, noticed and subsequently removed a letter that could be readily seen. It was carefully wrapped in clear plastic and addressed to Mr and Mrs Alderuccio, together with a framed child's drawing that could also be viewed within. The letter took Bron's notice because it was addressed directly to us, and because it said that the author of the letter and her young daughter had been the last people to see the boys immediately after the accident, just prior to the fire consuming the car.

Bron and I had previously worked together at The Ark clothing stores, and I had no idea that her daughter, Lexie, had been going out with Raph. It is truly amazing how we are all very connected in so many convoluted ways and how these connections, whether they be obvious or hidden, play out.

Bron was at the accident site with Lexie when she noticed the letter addressed to us, and she knew that someone had to get it to us. She picked it up and then made a phone call to another old work friend of mine, Joni, also from my Ark association. Joni had wisely called the phone number left on the letter to ensure we were not dealing with a nutter or someone strange, which would have been so upsetting for all of us. Friends went to great lengths to protect us all from any further unwarranted trauma and we were so very grateful.

After an initial phone chat it was apparent to Joni that the letter had been written by a very legitimate and caring woman who certainly meant no harm. She only wanted to help, and help she did. This strange link of past workmates and friends continued, as Joni contacted yet another old friend of ours, Mary. We had indeed also worked together previously at The Ark, but our friendship went way back to kinder days at St Brendan's and at Flemington Primary, where Carla and Mary's daughter, Brianagh, had been friends and in the same year. Both Joni and Mary arrived at our home together to deliver the plastic-wrapped letter, and my two friends explained to me how this amazing package had come to be.

It was the oddest of circumstances, and yet the most compelling of letters to read, and it came from a complete stranger named Jill. Although Jill and her three-year-old daughter, Evie, were both extremely traumatised over what they had witnessed only days before, it was so important for Jill to let us know that none of the boys was either visibly conscious or suffering as the fire took hold of the car. She happened to be driving past as the fire started in the boot area and must have missed the moment of actual impact only by seconds. It was a total blessing for them both, not to have witnessed that as well.

The letter's clear protective envelope contained a small framed drawing, courtesy of Evie, depicting Sam looking very peaceful, smiling and looking as if asleep, wearing his favourite red tee shirt. It may sound quite macabre and distressing that the drawing was done and subsequently delivered to us, but it helped little Evie identify and cope with what she had just witnessed. We somehow, inexplicably, also understood this completely, and were extremely grateful to have her incredibly kind gift.

Some weeks later, after Sam's funeral, Sergio and I made contact with Jill and we decided to all meet for coffee. Fate truly had stepped in that day on 3 May 2012. Jill was able to tell us she felt that all three boys had just passed away at that very moment as she and Evie slowly drove past, on their way to Evie's kindergarten. No one else was on the road at that exact time, in that exact spot: it was just Sam, Raph, Jesse, Jill and Evie on Westgarth Street. According to Jill, the crash scene looked so absolutely calm, serene and strangely non violent.

She believes, and I agree with her, that all three boys had passed away together, at the precise time that she and Evie slowly went past, and thanks to her we know that none of our sons suffered at all or were struggling to escape the fire. News such as this does make a massive difference, as it removes so many horrible possibilities going through so many minds. Tragically the final outcome is still the same, but knowing that they did not suffer absolutely means so very much to everyone.

Mother's Day fell only about ten days after the accident, and on that day we had a visit in the morning from two beautiful brothers, Luke and Yano, who came bearing gifts for me from them both and also lovingly on Sam's behalf. It was such a kind, generous and humane gesture, and also a very emotional one for all of us. Both Carla and Sam have the most amazing friends, who are compassionate, understanding and not afraid of showing raw human emotions. They are beautiful qualities to have that will serve them all well on their own journey through life.

The three of us went out for lunch at Pinotta, in Fitzroy North. Sergio and Carla wanted to acknowledge Mother's Day on my behalf, which I really appreciated. It occurred to me that we had not really left the house for ten days straight, other than twice visiting the accident site on Westgarth Street, once all together and another time quietly with just me and my girlfriend, Jenny.

It was a difficult lunch to say the very least, with all of us trying to be strong and positive for one another yet knowing that all of our hearts were breaking for Sam to somehow be there with us, alive and well. Tears were never far away. We tried to be happy on some level, but it truly was an impossible option that day.

After leaving the restaurant to drive home to Flemington, Sergio just happened to turn the car around in Carlton to show us something. I can still see the massive rainbow in the sky behind us in Fitzroy North, from where we had just come. It was such a beautiful sign of hope and happiness. We all smiled and commented, Carla took a photo and we drove home, where we then put a sign on our front gate asking for no visitors that day.

As much as it was a wonderful comfort to us all, it was also difficult to find time to think, truly grieve and to write our eulogies dedicated to Sam. We now had a funeral date and a deadline to work towards. That was the day we three penned our words. I clearly remember sitting down at my laptop having absolutely nothing to offer, and yet I had so much to say.

We went our separate ways in the house that night to write our words for Sam, the hardest written task I have ever had to undertake. It would have certainly been no easier for Carla or Sergio.

CHAPTER 5

Funeral and memorial services

The absolutely only positive thing about having the coroner involved in Sam's passing was the fact that we had lots of time to prepare a very fitting and well thought-out service and subsequent celebration for him. We had thirteen days between the accident on 3 May and Sam's farewell on 16 May.

Sam was never a religious person himself, and I can distinctly remember only about a year before he passed we were chatting about many things. Then Sam, out of nowhere, asked if I believed in God. This was a very left of field question but he obviously had his reasons for asking it, whether they were apparent to him or not at the time.

I answered that I did in fact believe in God, and in typical Sam fashion he responded with, 'Bullshit, you never go to church.' I explained that to me, believing in God had nothing to do with going to church, it was about my own personal beliefs. I added that I said a prayer each day for my family and friends, for myself and for all the things we have been blessed with in this life.

Well, Sam was absolutely gobsmacked; he had no idea that this was my reality. Then things became really interesting. Sam wanted to know if I had ever seen the movie *Ghost*. Yes, I had, and I also added that I loved it. Sam at that time was working after school at the local Video Ezy store and we agreed that he and I would watch *Ghost* together in the coming week.

We had our DVD night together, just us. I have no idea where Sergio and Carla were; it seemed to be for whatever reason a night that just Sam and I were meant to share alone together.

Ghost is about the sudden and traumatic death of Sam Wheat, the main character played by Patrick Swayze, and his subsequent survival in spirit form until he is ready to cross over into the afterlife. For me the afterlife was a given, but for Sam this was something so very new and clearly something he had never really thought about, let alone discussed with his mum.

I realise it will seem very much out of context mentioning *Ghost* right here, but it is very important for later happenings in this book so here it has to stay.

It's truly unbelievable the amount of care and consideration that special friends will go to during these times of chronic despair. Carla had a visit from two beautiful friends from her Flemington Primary School days, a brother and a sister, who arrived at our home the day after the accident. Both had ever so thoughtfully put together a list of potential venues at which to hold Sam's memorial service. It took so much of the stress, anguish, emotion, time and effort away from us in searching for ourselves where we should hold Sam's service. We are forever grateful to John and Jess for taking the time to do this.

Carla had made it quite clear to us from the beginning that Sam would be requiring a very big and public venue in which to farewell him. How big is big? This was new to us. Sam was extremely popular, yes, but he was also only nineteen years old. How many friends can you make in that time? 'Plenty', was the answer, and we once again allowed our twenty-year-old daughter to guide us in deciding where we would remember and celebrate her brother's short but extremely busy life.

The most fitting of choices was eventually made, it being decided that Sam's last party of parties would be held in the Celebrity Room at the Moonee Valley Racecourse. It held seven hundred people seated and another three hundred standing. I remember thinking that was one hell of a space to fill!

Now, as you will have seen from the previous paragraphs, Sam and religion were not that well acquainted. Both children were christened in the Catholic church, but if I am to be completely honest this was only so we could leave our options open as to what secondary school they might attend. The Catholic school system preferred their intake to be baptised within their own church, so we kept this door open as an option. I was christened Church of England, but to me religion is not about the 'brand' of the church or place of worship, it is simply about believing that there is a God or greater energy of some description.

Sergio's father was totally anti-religion, because in his mind God and the church failed to provide or protect him and his family in poverty-stricken Sicily during the depression of the

1930s and the Second World War. As a result, Nonno decided that his own children would not be exposed to the evils and inadequacies of the church. Never mind that Sergio's mother was a practising Catholic and a very religious woman throughout her lifetime, until she passed away aged only forty-four after years of ill health tracing back to contracting tuberculosis while growing up in Sicily.

I am not about to turn this book into a religious quest; it certainly is not that. I am just trying to explain our own dilemma around how we would arrange Sam's actual funeral service as opposed to the memorial service, which seemed to be way more straightforward and much more of a celebration of Sam's life.

Given that St Brendan's Catholic Church had baptised both Carla and Sam, we felt that it was only fitting Sam be properly blessed and that we have some religious flavour added to the service that Sergio, Carla and I had painstakingly planned. In the end, Sam was farewelled privately in one of the lovely chapels at Fawkner Crematorium. Carefully chosen music was played, beautiful words were spoken and appropriate prayers were offered.

Everything was a bit of a paradox on that day of 16 May 2012. Our beautiful son, Sam, a religious non-believer, was being blessed by a Catholic priest and then cremated, even though the church does not fully condone, let alone recommend, the practice of cremating passed souls. At least Sam would have been in full agreement that his memorial service and subsequent wake afterwards were being held at a race track.

As things turned out, I actually believe Sam would have been very much in favour of the few but pertinent words Father Max spoke that day, as they were very carefully chosen, heartfelt, beautifully delivered and ever so relevant to Sam. We all appreciated this very much. Our small and intimate private service for Sam could not be kept to under ninety-six invitees and it broke my heart to see four of his young teenage mates, his uncle Carl and a family friend carry his coffin into the chapel together.

This may seem strange to some and perfectly normal to others, but I was so very much aware of Sam's presence that day, just as I have been ever since his passing. Yes, I was painfully aware of the highly polished timber coffin and the huge floral arrangement of white tulips that covered the casket like a blanket, but I knew deep within myself that the very essence of Sam was right there, so very close to us, and had not disappeared into the bowels of the building to be turned to ash.

For me the actual funeral and cremation were without a doubt the hardest part of the day, or of any day of my life for that matter, and I was truly grateful when that component was over. Many of us regrouped back at Robert and Nadine's home in Moonee Ponds for sandwiches, tea, coffee, wine and whatever else might settle the emotions. It was here that stories, little by little, started to be told. At first our family and friends, including the teenage ones, were apprehensive about saying Sam's name too loudly. They didn't want to upset us, but we actually wanted to hear Sam's name being used and we wanted to hear the stories that everyone seemed to have within them. It broke the ice, somehow making it easier for everyone to cope. Small ripples of laughter finally started to burst out; funny tales were in endless supply. I could have stayed there for so much longer, just listening and reminiscing.

It was time to go to the next part of this marathon day, Sam's memorial service in the Celebrity Room at the Moonee Valley Racecourse. It was overwhelming to arrive at the venue to see the parking places filling and people still appearing from everywhere.

All of the arrival music and the hundreds of family photographs that had been so carefully selected by us three were ready to roll, Sam's life in pictures about to be shared. Carla and her friend, Luke, had done an amazing job of dealing with these technical requirements that Sergio and I were so clueless about. Through beautifully chosen music that Sam loved, they had managed to set the tone. They had created a certain energy and mood to this huge room that made it feel very composed, definitely sad, and yet strangely filled with anticipation of what was to come.

As we and all of our extended family and friends arrived to occupy many of the first and second row seats immediately in front of the stage, the sheer impact of numbers was apparent. Every one of the seven hundred seats was occupied, and another three hundred wonderful people stood at the back and waited. The Celebrity Room was perfect. It was Sam's day, it was his time to shine and be remembered with both tears and laughter: one nineteen-year-old boy and a thousand people to pay their final respects to him and to us. When I think about it, it still has the capacity to both lift and break my heart.

Our very good family friend, Paul Newman, was kind enough to MC the service. Things had been carefully scripted and sorted well before the day. Because of the circumstances in which Sam passed we had more time to spend on the actual farewell, the celebration of the life that was, and we wanted so very much to honour Sam in the best way we possibly could. We had spent many hours at home going through our thousands of photographs and choosing as many as possible of Sam, to run as a backdrop on the large screens during the dialogue. The speeches were to last approximately one hour in total and Sam's image was to stay up for exactly seven seconds per photograph. I never took my eyes off those photos, even though I have seen them countless times before, but I also still clearly heard every single word being said by our family members and both our friends and Sam's in their wonderful eulogies.

Absolutely beautiful words and memories were shared by everyone who stood on the stage to remember Sam. Somehow Sergio managed to go first, followed by Carla, then family members spoke of their much-loved and adored nephew. Sam's friends told both lovely and lively stories about past antics and adventures, many of which we were clueless about until that day.

It was here that we found out how Sam got the nickname of 'Da Vinci', courtesy of his friend from Wesley, Lorenzo. Thanks to a neighbourhood mate, Billy, we learnt that Sam was more into graffiti than we first thought. He had yet another alias, the name 'Clerk', which will become very pertinent as we continue through the chapters of this book.

My words came last. I never intended to voice them myself, as it was way beyond my emotional capabilities. My gorgeous friend, Leanne, who I met during my own kindergarten days in Tatura circa 1964, stood with her lovely husband, Michael, and told our story, Sam's story.

Throughout this amazing service, I can remember not crying much. I felt Sam's presence so strongly, and I knew he was somehow washing over me an unseen strength that I had never really felt with such intensity before. I could greet people, talk, laugh and even give them tissues to stem their own tears. It was like I had been given some kind of elixir that gave me an inner knowing and fortitude that certainly did not come from within the normal me.

We really wanted to properly celebrate Sam's life that day, and to do that we needed to put on a party. The Celebrity Room slowly cleared and everyone went into the huge bar area for sandwiches, copious beers, wines, tea, coffee and soft drinks. For me, it was as if Sam was walking right there beside me, I felt his presence that strongly. When friends commented on how steely and in control I appeared, I remember telling them that Sam was with me and giving me his strength. Probably daunting information for some, but it was my reality.

James, Michael, Lorenzo and Gussy in front of a 'Da Vinci' piece, 2018

A friend of ours, obviously someone with a good clear mind and foresight, had suggested we buy and lay out loads of loose paper sheets and pens on a designated table and ask everyone to write a message to Sam, or to us, anything at all of their own choosing. It was such a wonderful idea, and we now have hundreds of heartfelt and moving pages that have been carefully put away, with the condolence cards and small notes from the floral tributes. In time, when I can face organising it, these will all be bound into a book to keep within the family to last throughout the ages.

On this day another thing occurred to us: where did all these hundreds and hundreds of young people come from? When we asked this question of the many young friends we did actually know, they said that Sam knew everyone from everywhere, he had many circles of friends, lots who did not know one another, but there was a common denominator and it was always Sam. Everyone knew him!

Sam had a way about him that enabled him to bring together so many people from all walks of life, from all levels of education and from all sorts of cultures. He judged no one, and he had within him the amazing ability to blend and immerse different friends within different groups. Many still tell us that without Sam they would never have met certain people or had the opportunity to become part of the fold or to feel included, both at school and in lifelong friendship groups formed since.

It's a beautiful quality to have and it makes us feel so proud that Sam created an amazing legacy in such a short amount of years. It was also not lost on Sergio, Carla and I, that also present at Sam's service were his two kindergarten teachers from St Brendan's, every single teacher that ever taught him at Flemington Primary School, including both principals past and present, and at least a dozen teachers from Wesley College, including his senior school principal. Sam's Uncle Rob always likened Sam's many friendship groups to being like the Olympic rings, linking many groups together and are all totally encompassing with each other. It is a very apt description, I say.

Party time with Wesley crew

Sam and Wesley friends in Thailand, 2012

Sam and Wesley friends in Thailand, 2012

Caulfield, Sam and Liv at Wesley Valedictory dinner in 2011

CHAPTER 6

Moving forward

Many of us have read, heard or experienced first hand how after someone passes the many friends and casual visitors just gradually stop visiting. They all understandably need to get on with their own, largely intact lives and allow you to try to retie together the threads of your own. Thankfully, for us this never happened, our friends and Sam's kept on visiting and the strength and happiness that this gave us was immeasurable.

I slowly tried to sort through Sam's bedroom, which was not an easy feat for two main reasons. The first was the fact that it was so emotionally impossible to be upstairs among Sam's personal treasures and childhood keepsakes. The second was that Sam never kept the cleanest or tidiest of rooms, it being described as extremely shambolic and homely all in one.

Sam was the prince of tee shirts: he loved them and had masses of choices in varying degrees of disrepair, sizes, styles and colours. I decided to wash them all and give one to each of his family members and to his friends as they popped over for a visit, meal or beer or just for a chat. There were around fifty tee shirts to share, and I was once again very grateful to Sam for hoarding these treasures in his room. We of course kept some favourites for ourselves. It's hard to express how so many happy memories were sparked by simple cotton tee shirts that had been worn by Sam with so much gusto and love of life.

The truly amazing thing about Sam's friends, both male and female, was that they were all so loyal to him, to one another and to us. I know that they still keep in touch with Raph's family, which is wonderful to know, and Jesse's mates do the same thing with his family. It makes me very happy to know that we all have the love and support of these gorgeous young people and they have ours. I think the sudden and totally unexpected passing of the boys really took its toll on all who knew them, and a special kind of bond was formed and kept to support one another.

I was often asked by family and friends how we all managed to cope with Sam's passing and how we kept going each and every day. The answer was easy to give: we absolutely had no choice. We just had to endure and be there for one another and try to reconnect with our previous lives, ones that had been brutally changed so suddenly.

Friends would ask me, 'Why are you going back to work?' My simple answer was, 'What else am I supposed to do?' I had to be somewhere, I couldn't just hide and not be a part of life any more. I found this option to be a hideous possibility and, yet, I was asked so often how I could and would re-enter life.

It's really difficult to put into words, as mere words lack the emotion that was felt by us. I don't dare try to speak for Sergio and Carla, or anyone else for that matter, as to how they managed to cope each day with moving forward. It's such a personal thing, which we all have to handle in our own way. Some days were good ones, no tears or melt downs in either public or behind closed doors. Others were torturous, as you are somehow reminded every minute of the day of your deep-rooted sense of loss and pain. You are grief stricken, powerless, weak, fragile, lost and yet so very present in this living hell, which has replaced what was once a wonderful life.

We all have different emotions, varied ways of expressing ourselves; we can't possibly all react the same way. For me, I always had hope. I knew that things just had to get better, not just for me but also for my family. You absolutely cannot remain in a place so low and absent of happiness, it's just not possible; things had to get better. Just as hot air, the sun and the moon always rise, our emotions had to lift as well and, in time, they did.

Please don't think it all happens in alignment with some type of crazy unseen timeline, because it just doesn't. As I write these words, I can still be reduced to tears in a nanosecond, triggered by certain memories about Sam or my beautiful dad, who also left my life way too soon. We are never meant to forget our loved ones. They are a part of us, a part of our own DNA.

It is my own personal belief that the soul always survives that protected me from feeling the blackest and most empty of pains that I know so many people do endure. I have seen first hand that when people believe their loved ones are forever gone and truly dead they can see nothing beyond this black hole of extermination. For them there is no hope, no bright side to anything, and their pain manifests itself into something so tangible and consuming that happiness can no longer be an option. I have never accepted physical death as anyone's ending. For me, all passed souls reside in the afterlife, on another plane, in another dimension, but never far away.

A month after the accident I reluctantly returned to work at our restaurant. It was so difficult going back that very first day. Sergio drove me in and two of my girlfriends came down during lunch service to make sure I was okay with being out in the wider public again. The other amazing thing was that each and every business owner I knew along the laneway came to offer their condolences to me in person. I was so touched and forever grateful for being a part of this tiny little hospitality community in the heart of the city. We still have a huge daphne bush on our balcony that was delivered to Amigos during this time, courtesy of the business owners along the laneway. You don't ever tend to forget such things.

Another strange and wonderful thing began to happen each day after lunch service finished: the lovely young staff from all of the surrounding restaurants started coming to Amigos. We would sit together outside in the winter chill and chat and laugh and just be together. Sam's name was rarely mentioned, but I knew it was because of him that they came. It was like the United Nations, with gorgeous young men and women predominantly from the United Kingdom, Europe and Asia coming in each day to just eat, drink and be together.

They felt my pain. Most were not that well known to me, let alone to my family, and only a few had met Sam, yet these beautiful people came to show their respect, support and love, because at the end of the day we are all sons, daughters, mothers, fathers, brothers, sisters and, ultimately, human beings.

Two lovely English boys, Seb and Matt, became very close to me, and even asked that I become their Australian mum while they lived out their dream stay for two years here in Australia. I gratefully accepted and ended up being privy to way too much information regarding their love life conquests and relationship dramas. They seemed to share much more with me than they would with your average mum, and we all laughed as I failed miserably in trying to keep them both on the straight and narrow.

Tragically, Matt had also suffered a huge loss at a young age, having lost his own mother to a terminal illness not long before arriving in Melbourne. It was so sad for him, at only twenty-one years of age. The night before Sam's accident, Matt and I had a very teary heart to heart in our upstairs bar about how much he missed not having his own mum there in his everyday life. I truly hope that I offered him the warmth and compassion he truly deserved and was of comfort to him in some way, just as he has since been to me.

Seb, Matt and their boss, Leo, from the restaurant opposite to ours all attended Sam's memorial service wearing their crisp, newly purchased white shirts, and they offered me much love and support just by being there. I have never forgotten this kind deed, and I think our continued daily hugs thereafter were a lovely sharing of mutual affection between a surrogate mum and her temporary sons, each a stand-in for those who could not be physically present.

On many fabulous occasions I also had visits to Amigos from a multitude of Sam's wonderful friends. They would book a big table and I would sit and join them for drinks and a meal after my shift finished. They would all have dinner together, eating, drinking and laughing as I watched on. I absolutely loved being with them all afterwards, just me and Sam's friends.

I am eternally thankful we got to share these very special catch ups, and at other times just one or two of Sam's friends would call past and we would share a nice lunch or after work tipple. I didn't care what time of day or night it was, I just wanted to spend time with each and every one of them.

Wesley mates and me at Amigos, 2012

CHAPTER 7

The lights at Farnham Street

A few strange things started to happen with the lights at home immediately after Sam's passing. Prior to the funeral, whenever we knew that Sam's friends were coming over, which was thankfully often and usually in the early part of the evening, I would turn on the house lights as dusk descended.

Our home was an old Victorian one with very high ceilings, and more lights than normal were needed to illuminate the adjoining kitchen and dining room properly. In those rooms we had five sconces spread around the walls and one pendant light in each respective area. I would turn the lights on and invariably two or three light globes would blow out all at once. This was an absolute first, and I found it amazing and also quite exciting.

To me it was a message, a sense of knowing on Sam's part, that he was aware his friends would be arriving to visit us soon; this was his way of showing us that he knew what was happening. I can completely understand that some of you may find this a huge leap of faith, or even regard it as madness on my part, that I could construe blown light bulbs to be some kind of spiritual awareness or, dare I say, spiritual presence.

Point taken, but you could not ignore the forty plus light bulbs that blew out after Sam's passing, each and every time his friends came over to see us. The greater the number of visitors, the bigger the count of light globe fatalities. It was wonderful!

Our dining room light took things to a new level of paranormal possibilities, when we inadvertently discovered that once we turned it off at the switch the light would come back on, ever so gently at first, and it would then pulsate. I'm not sure which one of us discovered this phenomenon, but it was a bit of a game changer for all of us. We then noticed that the light started to react to our own emotional moods. When there was lots of emotional upset in the house, which was quite often, the light, although switched off, would flash quite violently, on and off, on and off. The gentle pulsating light experienced when things were calm was replaced by a change of tempo that mirrored the feelings of those of us at home that night.

The energy of the dining room light was truly remarkable and we were thankfully able to demonstrate this strange happening to visiting family and friends as well, which was a blessing. It would have been very easy to believe we had all experienced some form of mental melt down, had others not witnessed it as well. All we had to do was turn the light switch off, leave the room and stand in the hallway. When we popped our heads back into the room to look at the light, it would start to faintly go back on and then off. The more intense the mood, the stronger the light was. It got to a stage that I loved standing in the hallway, just watching the reflection from the doorway of the light going on and off at will above the dining room table.

I honestly believed, and I still do, that we had made a connection with Sam through pure energy, albeit an unusual one, that we were actually communicating with one another.

The incredible thing was that Sam also managed to bring this priceless gift of electrical manipulation to our new home in Fitzroy North, in March the following year. On the very first night that some of his friends visited us in our new townhouse one of the bathroom downlights blew out just before their arrival. It was only for about an hour, and then it started to automatically work again later on. Brilliant!

Farnham Street home

Sergio and me with some of the boys, Gussy, Lorenzo and Todd

Christine, me, Sam, Carla and Anna in Positano, Italy in 2010

CHAPTER 8

Dreams and visits

Earlier on I wrote about having a disturbing dream the night before Sam's accident, which turned out to be an incredibly accurate premonition, somehow intertwined into my dream time. What I have found throughout my lifetime, and in the past five years especially, is that sometimes there are no easily explainable answers or reasons for what's happening in your world. Things just happen, and the best lesson I have learnt is to let them unfold and see what comes of it.

From a really young age of around five or six years, I can still clearly remember thinking you could not ever possibly die. To me it was impossible. I was curiously so very much aware of this small voice that lived within me, and I just knew nothing could ever stop this inner 'me' from surviving forever. I also had a fascination with the word 'infinity', although I struggled to grasp its actual meaning and I still do. For me it was just instinctively knowing that these two moments of enlightenment, never dying and infinity, were completely and totally linked together and would one day become clear to me.

Dreams for me were usually fantastic experiences, in which I could go anywhere or be anything. My favourite ones were those in which I could fly. I found I could conjure up any topic and invariably would be able to dream about things I wanted to. I was even able to continue with the same dream the next night if it had been cut short because of morning dawning, bringing about my own untimely consciousness. I loved being able to do this and thought it was the norm for everyone.

Over the years my dreams have expanded their themes, and my nights of flying, with arm movements resembling swimming freestyle in mid-air, have become something way more significant and influential to my life.

I started to have visits from my loved ones in the spirit world, certainly not every night or even every month, but drop-in visits they were. I loved it when this happened. They were unlike normal dreams, where you wake up knowing strange things have taken place but you can't actually fully remember what they were. With these 'dreams' I would wake up remembering every single detail of my loved ones being with me, and there was always a message or piece of advice that stayed with me until the next morning and usually well beyond.

The messages were invariably of real significance to what was happening in my world at that time, and it never failed to give me clarity and guidance in going forward with my life. Of course, I always felt utter, extreme and immense happiness after these dream visits, and I longed for them to be of a more regular nature.

By the time I reached fifty-three years of age I had experienced many hours of beautiful family visits while in the dream state. By then I had lost my son, father, two grandmothers, two grandfathers, step-brother, two step-grandfathers, close relatives, family friends and countless family pets to the afterlife, and my dreams kept me very much connected with them all.

I was secretly anticipating and yet was not fully prepared for how I would cope with Sam's first dream visit to me. I instinctively knew it would happen, but beyond that I just had to wait and see. When the dream did occur it happened without any real fuss or fanfare on Sam's part, which on reflection is pretty much typical of how Sam did things. He was just there as per normal, with Sergio, Carla and me all having a meal together.

What was incredibly special was that he was wearing a tee shirt with an infinity symbol on it! This was my 'forever' symbol, which I had seen since childhood, and this further validated that Sam was truly visiting me from the afterlife. It was such a game changer. The whole experience was so wonderful, the dream was so full of love and hope, I remember waking up in tears but also feeling fantastic at the same time.

In another of my dreams Sam thought he was just silently and invisibly visiting me as I slept, but I was able to tell him I could actually see him. He was shocked by this phenomenon, and it was the real beginning of us both understanding that we could and actually were making contact with one another. Words cannot express how I felt after this remarkable experience.

After this, Sam started to pop in on a more regular basis. Sometimes he would present himself as an older teenager, looking closer to his nineteen years, and at other times he would look to be aged under ten or even be of kindergarten age. Sam seemed to have complete control over how old he wanted to look at any particular time. I was amazed and started to love going to sleep each night, just to see what would happen.

These dream visits always coincided with something very significant happening in our lives, and without fail two outcomes occurred. One, I would always wake knowing what to do about a certain situation, and two, I would feel a real sense of calm about me and with my life in general.

They are to me, without a doubt, visits from Sam and also from my many loved ones. I so hope that all of you reading my words will be lucky enough, if you haven't already been, to have some of these amazing experiences as well. Please don't doubt their validity, they are real and they are messages and experiences meant just for you.

CHAPTER 9

Seeing a medium

It was Sergio's sister, Diana, who first mentioned the word 'medium' to me. Her second cousins had been seeing various mediums over the years, since the untimely and early passing of their beautiful mother, Carmel, from breast cancer. These mediumship readings seemed to bring much peace to the girls, and apparently lots of amazing evidence of survival was communicated between this world and the next.

Because of this Diana went to see a woman called Lillian in Melbourne's northern suburbs, and the results she reported back to me were astounding. There were messages from Maria and from Diana, Sergio and Robert's late mother, who I sadly never had the opportunity to meet. She had passed away with a combination of illnesses at the age of forty-two years, when Diana was nine, Robert thirteen and Sergio sixteen.

This was incredible news to me, that contact with spirit was being made via a stranger. How could this be? When Diana told me that Sam came through as well I was utterly astonished, but when I look back I'm really not sure why I found this phenomenon to be so implausible. I had always believed in the afterlife and survival of the soul, and now I was being presented with my own opportunity to explore what seemed to many people to be impossible. I was feeling very excited!

All of my life, I have perceived the presence of spirit around me. They were not felt all of the time, of course, but often when I was lying in bed at night I would feel a real change in the energy of the room. Many times I felt someone lay down beside me or I would feel the bed depress, as if someone had just sat by my side. This is strangely something that I have always found extremely comforting and peaceful. I spoke inside my mind to these visitors, who were invariably family and friends who loved dearly and missed deeply.

Communication between the two worlds was always in my belief system, and indeed a reality to me. What did blow my mind was that a complete stranger, this person called a medium, could also join the party!

Sergio and Carla had decided to take a more conventional approach to try to deal with their own respective sense of loss, and both had separately started to attend grief counselling sessions provided by the Traffic Accident Commission (TAC). I can't say why, simply that I have no answer, but this path had no appeal to me at all. Having said this, I also knew I was desperate to seek some form of help and reassurance from someone, anyone, that Sam was still okay and that, in time, I would be too.

During a quiet time at Amigos, I started googling the word 'medium' on my iPad. I had no idea what or who I was looking for, I just knew that I had to search for an answer. A name and associated website stood out from all the other contenders and I decided to make a call. Something told me I needed to be as anonymous as possible when making my enquiry and subsequent booking, as I wanted to know for certain that this woman knew absolutely nothing about me or my family. If Sam truly was there waiting to communicate from the spirit world, I wanted the medium to have a completely blank canvas with which to work.

My decision was made and the date was set to meet with Lorraine Culross, on 18 June 2012 at 2.00 pm at her home in the south-eastern suburbs of Melbourne. I went home that night and told Sergio and Carla what I had done. Both looked and sounded quite surprised, but I was totally unfazed. I knew I had to do this. Mediumship consultations were certainly not on either's radar, and I knew they were concerned about what I was about to do.

Sergio kindly asked if he could join me, just to make sure I would be all right and not end up leaving more upset than I was on arrival. I agreed, and I also very much appreciated him doing this, as I knew he was way out of his own comfort zone. I rang Lorraine to ask if my husband could join me for the reading. She was absolutely fine with this, she just wanted me to know that if I had any secrets from him they might come out during the session. No issues there, but this certainly made me even more curious about what we were going to experience.

A compromise was made between Sergio and me, that prior to our visit with Lorraine I would attend a grief counselling session at TAC with him. I agreed, and I could not wait for 18 June to arrive. On the morning of what was to become an absolute turning point in my life I spoke to Sam, as I had every single day since his passing, and as always I felt his presence around me and, more importantly, felt his love.

I remember telling him that Dad and I were seeing a medium called Lorraine at 2.00 pm that day. I hastened to add that I really had no idea what a medium actually did, but I needed Sam to be at the Aspendale Gardens address at this time. I also entrusted him with the actual street number!

Although the grief counsellor was a lovely, warm and compassionate woman, I remember sobbing my way through the entire session. When it finally ended I was left feeling an even greater sense of loss, as nothing was ever mentioned about Sam's eternal life, the afterlife or the survival of spirit. I understand that TAC grief counselling has its place and purpose, and for many I'm sure it helps them enormously.

Obviously, the TAC counsellors are not supposed to adopt my own personal beliefs of an eternal life. Theirs is more a textbook approach, concerning getting your own life back on track and moving forward one day and one step at a time. The session went against every belief and inner knowledge I possessed, and the endorsement of absolute annihilation of our loved ones did not sit well with me at all. I left the office feeling utterly devoid of any hope of happiness for the future, because apparently TAC's policy is that death is final and that person is no more.

Afterwards, Sergio and I drove southward to have a quiet lunch at the local Subway near Lorraine's home. We talked about the TAC session, and Sergio was not left wondering if I would be going back for another consultation. I was feeling so keyed up, both apprehensive and yet excited all at once. I knew within my gut that an hour-long mediumship session absolutely had to be better and more uplifting than what I had endured in my earlier grief counselling session.

We arrived a little early at my insistence. I was feeling so desperate to get there, so we could see for ourselves what was about to unfold. While waiting in the car near Lorraine's home, looking like a pair of stalkers, we noticed a small woman who was walking two little dogs disappear into the house with Lorraine's street number on it. She looked so regular and normal, like an ordinary middle-aged woman who was conservatively dressed. There was no flamboyant floral kaftan, massive hoop earrings and obligatory head scarf finished off with a pair of Roman sandals – she was one of us. My hopes soared, that this was going to be amazing. I could feel it within myself.

At 2.00 pm we rang the doorbell and there she was again, this lovely-looking, friendly, suburban medium. After trips to the loo for both Sergio and myself, we were ready to start. Thankfully, Lorraine was kind enough to tell us a bit about herself, how mediumship ran in her family and how she had discovered her gift only about thirteen years previously. She also went on to say that today had been very different for her in many ways.

Apparently for Lorraine, spirit normally makes their presence known only as the 'sitters' arrive, that is, us. On this occasion, Lorraine felt a spirit with her from early in the morning, and they simply would not leave. They were waiting for their family to arrive; once again, it was us!

After handing me a pencil sketch on an A4 piece of paper, of a cherubic male baby face, Lorraine explained that this was a 'vision' she was shown by the waiting spirit, and if I did not recognise it immediately I would later on. At the time it did not mean anything to either of us, as there was so much nervousness and anticipation going on for us both we could not place the pencil-sketched portrait. I put it aside and waited for Lorraine to start the reading.

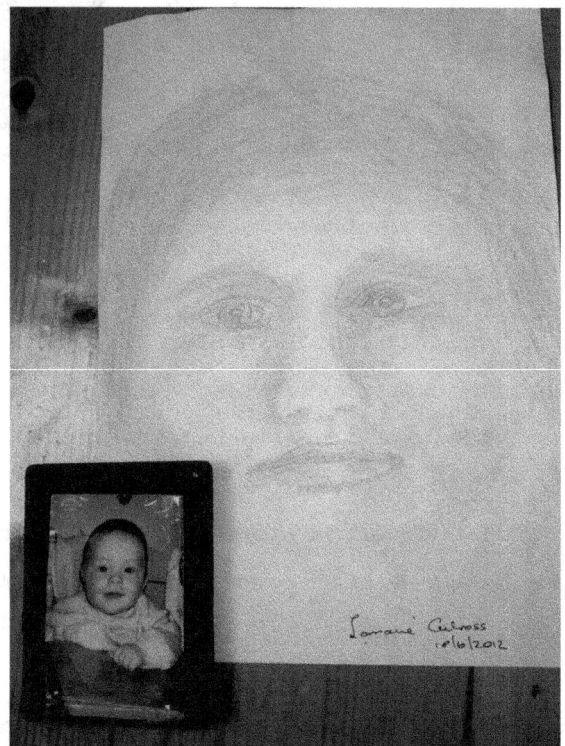

Spirit-inspired drawing by Lorraine Culross, June 2012

Lorraine's opening words were: 'You are a mother grieving the loss of your son, aged between eighteen and twenty years'. Well, the tears were back in full force, but unlike that morning's session these were tears of hope and joy and not of total despair. Sam was there to communicate with us via Lorraine, and had apparently been waiting ever since I asked him to be there that morning!

Lorraine also went on to say that Sam had been met by his grandfather, my father. At this early stage I could barely contain myself. There was also a small Italian woman in black with them. It was Sergio's mum, who passed away when he had been only sixteen years old. This was remarkable to us both, and we just sat and listened and cried.

Just weeks beforehand I had been given a beautiful silver bracelet with a small heart on it. One side said 'Sam' and the other 'Love J, J & B', a wonderful and very generous gift from Jen, John and Benjamin, long-term friends of ours. I had not taken it off since receiving it. Lorraine looked directly at me and pointed at my bracelet, then said that the bracelet had special significance in Sam's passing. This was amazing evidence for us both to hear and I couldn't wait to receive more.

Lorraine went on to say she could see a huge kind of race or running track and also lots of horses. We were both thrown off course a bit here, because Lorraine added that horses are symbolic of freedom and being free spirited. I remember commenting on how Sam liked to ride horses whenever the opportunity arose when he was younger, and that he was certainly free spirited, but that was all I could think to say at that moment.

You obviously need time to process what is being said at a reading at a later date, and thankfully the session was being recorded. It was only after I replayed the CD at home that I realised the communication Lorraine was receiving from Sam was actually about Moonee Valley Racecourse, where Sam's memorial service had been held! I cannot express how elated I felt, and also how stupid that this was not blatantly obvious to either of us on the day of the reading.

Without summarising the entire reading for you, I will just stay with the most relevant parts. Lorraine described my father's physical appearance exactly, and also added that he was a Rotarian and a man of immense integrity. He most certainly was, as he gave his own life trying to save the life of another. A full and correct description was also given of Sam, right down to his wonderful trademark smile, which could light up a room, and his beautiful bright eyes. The information kept on flowing, with Lorraine saying that Sam's second name was that of my father's. My dad was called James, and Sam was indeed Samuel James.

Lorraine knew that Sam was in two minds about attending university, and that he was wise beyond his years and had a beautiful soul: totally correct on every level. She described entering Sam's upstairs bedroom at Farnham Street, and upon opening the wardrobe doors she said, 'Chaos.' How true! Sam's cupboards took untidiness to great new heights, but as we had already started to discover for ourselves, when your life finds true perspective none of that futile stuff actually matters.

Sam's happy childhood was mentioned, and his riding a tricycle on the asphalt footpath we had in our street. Ours was not your regular modern concrete one. Lorraine talked about Sam kicking the footy on the roadway outside our home, and all the many opportunities he had been given in life. All of this was absolutely accurate, as was everything else she said.

Sam was in a bit of a quandary about life and was not sure what it was all about: he had trouble joining all the dots together at times. He also told Lorraine of wanting to work with the underprivileged and marginalised members of society. She said that the spiritual quality of Sam was great. We always felt he would become a teacher or social worker, so this was incredibly heartening for us to hear. Lorraine mentioned that Sam has a great sense of humour and was enjoying the intrigue of the reading very much. This did not surprise me for an instant!

Lorraine said that Sam's passing was over in an instant, there had been no pain and it took only a nanosecond. She said that one arm was not working, his left one, that he had been distracted while driving and had to steer with one arm.

Apparently, even after we left Lorraine's home, Sam would not leave. He kept 'telling' her he was distracted from the back seat just before the accident. She kindly rang us that night to tell us this, as it was quite obviously very important to Sam that we knew this. I remain so grateful to both Sam and Lorraine for sharing this information with us.

We both left Lorraine's home that afternoon feeling totally overwhelmed, absolutely blown away, and for me in particular so full of hope and wonderment of what just took place, and how this was going to transform my own future.

I asked Sergio what he made of the reading. I also enquired as to what he would have said if I had come home with all of this information without him being present to witness it for himself. He said very quickly, without the need to think any further, that I would be deemed to be completely mad and totally certifiable had he not been there. He added that he could not deny the wonder of it and would not attempt to. I am so pleased he was there to partake in this wondrous experience. Thanks to Lorraine and her amazing gift of mediumship, I found that day to be a healing experience that was stronger than anything I had ever experienced at that time.

Phil, me, Lorenzo, Sergio, and Carla out front of the amazing 'Da Vinci' piece, courtesy of Charlie Vaughan

CHAPTER 10

Hope ... and getting back to living

For me the visit to Lorraine was an absolute turning point. I am eternally grateful I chose to see her so soon after the accident, because she allowed me to understand that all I had ever believed in was true. Sam was still very much alive, as were all my loved ones. Not in the physical sense, however, the essence of them existed in spirit form and this was going to be enough for me.

I spoke cautiously at first to friends and family about Lorraine and the reading. Some people were wary, concerned even, and others were amazed and more curious than I could ever have imagined, and some had actually been to see mediums themselves. Why did I not know that these people existed?

I was so pleased our experience was with such a good medium, who was a kind and caring person. The reading had such a positive and direct impact on how we both started to cope with everyday life again from thereon. It was like a new world had been discovered by me, and previously closed doors started to open. I began what I now know was a healing process.

After speaking openly one night with Chico, a lovely host from one of the other restaurants in the laneway, he surprised me the next day with a big hard-cover book called *Conversations with God*, by Neale Donald Walsch. Well, at first I wasn't sure what to make of it, but the gesture was so kind I decided to read the book. I had never heard of this author, and to be totally honest most of the literary choices over my lifetime had always been embarrassingly one dimensional and very genre specific: mainly lightweight holiday reads by John Grisham, David Baldacci, Jeffrey Archer, Barbara Taylor Bradford, Wilbur Smith, J.K. Rowling and other prolific wordsmiths. Some are cringe-worthy choices in their own way, but these were my chosen books at that time. Up until then, I thought that together with these generic bestsellers and a large number of cookbooks in my personal collection I was fairly well read!

I also discovered that the volume I had on loan from Chico was one of many, apparently 'channelled' by Walsch directly from God. This was all a little daunting, and I even had to google exactly what channelling was all about. It was not a book I left lying about for all to see, at home or at work. I was unsure what others may think, and at this early stage I was a little uncertain about what I was going to make of it myself.

Clearly, I had many internal unspoken issues going on within myself. I did actually believe in a god, I always had, but this was information I didn't bandy around that freely, as previously noted by Sam's initial shock.

Discreetly, one day soon after I started reading Chico's book on the tram while heading into Amigos. I began work at noon, so I could always find an empty seat to read covertly as the tram was never packed at this late morning hour. Once I got used to how the book was laid out, literally Walsch speaking and then God replying, I really started to enjoy what was actually being said. The author was asking God no-nonsense questions about death and passing over into the spirit world, and God was giving some amazing and very interesting replies.

In many ways this book showed me there is so much more to life than what we just 'see'. We know so much about certain things in life, but in reality it's all so lopsided. We vaguely know how to navigate our way through what's known as 'living', as functioning human beings who seek education, work, travel, politics, family life, love, sport, the arts, whatever, but we rarely look beyond the tangibly obvious. This book did, and I loved what I found.

More books of this kind followed, and I am forever grateful to Chico for broadening my reading selections to a far greater and more empowering spread of literature. I started to discover entire new aisles and sections in book stores titled New Age, Religion or Spirituality. At first these were a tad too left of field for me, but I have to confess I have found incredibly helpful books in these sections. They resonated with me immediately, with what I was going through on a spiritual level at that stage of my life.

So much had happened for us in such a very short amount of time that year. I look back now and wonder how we coped and managed to do all that we did.

As I mentioned earlier we as a family have always loved to travel, and as Carla and Sam grew older they started to travel independently of us. This pleased us greatly. There is absolutely nothing that will educate you in the ways of the world and life as does travel. It broadens the mind, the heart and the soul. In my mind, there really is no substitute.

Sam and Carla in Italy, 2010

Carla made the decision, with our full support, not to continue her university studies for the year after Sam's passing. The opportunity presented itself for Carla to join her long-term boyfriend Paul in Amsterdam, where he was studying on an exchange program with Melbourne University. As sad as it was to see Carla fly to the other side of the world, we both fully understood her need to go and be with Paul, and to also be away from all the reminders of a life that once was. She was due to leave in October 2012.

At around the same time, Sergio and I received an invitation to attend the wedding of friends of ours, Carolyn and Tony, in Brooklyn, New York in August. We decided that if we were going to go that far we may as well include a week in Mexico, as Sergio had never been there before. I had visited the year before with the same Carolyn who was getting married and another friend, also called Carolyn, just prior to opening our Mexican restaurant in the city.

Everything was booked and away we went. The change of scenery did us both good, Mexico in particular. It was great to just be away from everything and to experience a new country together, and in many ways to try to refocus away from the months of upset and turmoil we had just been through. Sam was very much a part of this trip; I felt his presence and closeness. He was never far away, and he could return to me as quickly as it took to think his name.

I would have loved for the four of us to have been able to visit this beautiful and vibrant country at some stage, as both Carla and Sam would have enjoyed the culture, the people, the food, the wonderful scenery and history and, of course, the tequila!

I absolutely adore New York and, as already outlined, Sam and I had spent a fantastic week there, just us two, on our mother and son trip when he was only sixteen. It felt very bittersweet to be back there again without him, and I found myself often wandering around alone in the areas Sam and I had been to and loved most. His presence was very much felt by me in particular, and when Sergio and I heard Israel Kamakawiwo'ole's version of 'Over the Rainbow' through the sound system the very moment we walked into the Coffee Bean and Tea Leaf café, it absolutely blew me away. We played this unique version of this amazing song in the short and very carefully chosen play list at Sam's funeral at Fawkner Crematorium, and I have never heard it played anywhere else. Carla chose this cover of such a beautiful song, and to me this was a wonderful sign we were not alone in the Big Apple.

Sergio and I attended Carolyn and Tony's wedding in Brooklyn, a beautiful occasion and a lovely celebration of two very well-matched souls. We both enjoyed being distracted from the sad reminders of where our lives were at back home. But it was a temporary escape only, and we both knew it would only ever be that.

In our absence away from home, Carla and her dear friend Anna stayed together at Farnham Street to mind the cats and to be of support to one another. As we found out later, three of Sam's closest mates – Lorenzo, Charlie and Gussy – also stayed over most nights, with all of them reminiscing, laughing, no doubt crying and without a doubt partying. By this stage both girls had just turned twenty-one and the boys were a mix of eighteen and nineteen years. So much rapid growing up to do; no one asked if they were ready, they just had to be. The house and cats survived our absence and Carla said how fantastic it was to spend so much time with both hers and Sam's friends while we were away. We were very pleased they all stayed over, and Carla seemed a lot happier at last. We were both so relieved to see this positive change in her.

CHAPTER 11

Moving house

It was blatantly obvious from everything I had read that you supposedly shouldn't make too many, if any, bold and life-altering changes in the first one or two years after losing a loved one. This obviously went in one ear and out the other, as we decided to sell our beautiful family home. We had lived very happily in this home for the past twenty years, and it had been just four months since Sam's passing. It no longer truly felt like a family home any more, for we were one family member short.

I was working long hours and nights at Amigos. Carla was about to move to Amsterdam to be with Paul, and poor Sergio understandably hated the thought of just him being there alone, night after night, waiting for me to get home, by which time he was already asleep. The reality was it felt right for us to pack up and go, and I firmly believe that you only need to gauge your own feelings and subsequent actions. It can't always be so prescriptive to put timelines on things; life does not work that way. We three all knew we were ready to move on, and so we did.

The wheels were set in motion in September, with one of the local Flemington real estate agents being engaged to auction our fabulous home. So much to do, so much to sort, toss and pack. An auction date was set for 1 December 2012, and the marketing campaign started in earnest.

Carla was due to leave for The Netherlands in October, and the opportunity of a cycling trip to Sicily presented itself to Sergio. With much coercing from us, he finally decided to return to the homeland of his family to go riding with a few Melbourne friends. The plan was to enjoy the time cycling to and from ancient hilltop villages and then stay with his extended family when the ride was over. It then seemed a perfect idea for Carla to start her European sojourn a bit earlier, join her dad in Sicily after his ride and then continue on to meet Paul in Amsterdam and stay for the next five months.

During all the business of booking flights and accommodation for Carla and Sergio, we also started to look for a new place to call home. Carla and I asked Sergio where he would like to move to and he reeled off a very short list of suburb candidates from which to choose: Carlton, Carlton North, Fitzroy, Fitzroy North, or possibly over the river in Albert Park. All of these areas ticked my boxes as well, so that certainly narrowed things down somewhat.

Once again via Google I very quickly found us a brand new townhouse that had failed to sell at auction the week before. It was in a tiny development, only three townhouses in total, built on a wedge-shaped piece of land that had apparently once housed the local firewood merchant and his huge wood stack.

We are not a family that procrastinates over making decisions, and our new home on Alfred Crescent, Fitzroy North was first viewed four days before Sergio's cycling trip and purchased by me, in his absence, a week later.

This was both extremely exciting and also incredibly daunting, as there was so much to do in such a short amount of time prior to our 1 December house auction. We now had a moving date to work towards, mid-February 2013, after the settlement of Alfred Crescent.

We didn't follow one of the most basic rules of real estate, being sell first then buy. Yes, the proverbial cart had been put before the horse, and we really needed to sell Farnham Street in December and be ready to move out not that long afterwards.

At this time I could no longer put off properly sorting out Sam's bedroom. I had already dispersed his huge tee shirt collection to appreciative family and friends, but that truly was the very tip of a very big iceberg. Sam was more of a hunter and collector type, and not one to shed possessions easily. He had more things than I could believe possible squirrelled away in his very substantial wardrobe space. I refused to part with his myriad sentimental childhood trinkets, various school projects, other random clothing and his brand new Dom Bagnato suit, which Sergio had bought for him to wear to his Year 12 formal at Wesley College.

Sam looked so very handsome in his beautifully made charcoal grey suit, and I remember thinking when I first saw him wearing it that it fitted him so perfectly, and that it would never fit him again because, like all young men, he was still growing at a rapid rate of knots. As it turned out, Sam only ever got to wear his lovely suit that one and only time. It's almost as though it was the exact size for that precise and very perfect moment of time and it was never actually meant to be worn again. To this day it hangs with Sam's accompanying new shirt and tie in the guest room wardrobe at our new home, another happy/sad reminder of what was, and what can never be again.

Sam going to Wesley Year 12 formal, 2011

I could only cull and pack so much at this stage, because our home still had to look like people lived there in some degree of conformity and comfort and were not too obviously leaving any time soon. I did have the sense to realise that it's never good to have potential buyers know you really need to sell at auction, as your new abode clearly awaits.

The task of packing up was horrendous, not just in Sam's bedroom but in every room of our large and over-filled home. It wasn't a matter of just sorting out the excess possessions, it was also a matter of me knowing I would have to cull approximately seventy per cent of our total belongings in order to fit things into our comparatively tiny new townhouse.

Sergio came home from Sicily after a very enjoyable bike ride and a fantastic trip with Carla and her lovely friend Ally. Ally, also a Wesley friend, happened to be in Europe at the same time, so she was able to join both Sergio and Carla on visits to Sergio's relatives from both his parents' sides of our Sicilian family. According to Sergio, these visits were wonderful yet also very emotional, and often downright sad. All of the family had met Sam on more than a few occasions previously on family holidays, and our tragic loss was theirs as well.

I was grateful to have so much happening each and every day during this time, as it somehow faintly dulled the painful memory of once having two gorgeous teenagers living at home with us only months before. Inexplicably, now there were just us and the two cats, Megan and Jingles.

Regardless of all that needed to be done over the next few months, I was determined to spend time with both Carla and Paul in Europe between New Year and the time we had to move across town in mid-February. That old saying, 'Where there is a will, there is a way' became my mantra, and I booked my flights and accommodation in Copenhagen, Brussels, Antwerp, Bruges and Amsterdam. My decision was made, as I could not, and would not wait until the end of February for Carla to come home. I just knew I had to be with her at that time.

Auction day finally arrived on 1 December, and as luck would have it the generally buoyant Melbourne real estate market was taking a hit and now was not a great time to sell. The only saving grace was that we also had bought Alfred Crescent in the same market, so being the eternal optimist that I am, to my way of thinking all things evened out financially in the end. A local family with two young children acquired Farnham Street, and it pleased us all to know that another family would get to live in that wonderful old home filled with so many amazing memories.

The day the sale contracts were signed I went into total overdrive in regard to really starting to sort and pack twenty years of family life into a minimum of boxes, turfing unneeded or unsellable items and putting together huge amounts of furniture, books, kitchenware, ceramics, crockery, glassware, paintings, electrical goods and random stuff for hopeful sale at an upcoming garage sale, scheduled straight after I got back from Europe.

In early January 2013, I left Sergio and the two cats to their own devices and flew to Copenhagen to meet up with Carla and Paul, who had been holidaying and celebrating Christmas and the new year in Berlin. My motherly withdrawals were temporarily satisfied, I finally had my 'fix' of being reunited with our beautiful daughter. Paul had to leave for Amsterdam after two days of fun and sightseeing in stunning Copenhagen, as he had to continue with his studies at university. Carla and I headed off to Belgium a day or so later, where we caught up with Seb, my English surrogate son, and I finally got to meet his wonderful mum, Brigitte. Seb always said that we would get along famously, and he was so right!

Carla and I had the time of our lives being away together. It gave us a chance to reconnect with one another, and we both loved the opportunity of having this beautiful one-on-one experience. Sam's name was used lovingly and often, always linked with happy memories of our family trips away in the past or just recalling the funny everyday things he did that made us all laugh. We didn't dare go any deeper than this, for neither of us was ready to discuss our future lives at home without Sam being physically there with us. We kept our conversations and memories at surface level, as the rawness of grief was never far away, and I realise now that we both just wanted to be happy and absorbed in one another's company.

We couldn't change our lives; we could only enjoy and embrace the now, and the 'now' was fun at that time. Being together away from the realities of home gave us both a false yet satisfying sense of security, in not having to face the harsh facts of what life now was for us all. As with Sam, being together with Carla was a perpetual easy joy and we had, and still do have an effortless ability to truly just enjoy one another's company.

As I said earlier, our home in Flemington was always the party house, the place where all the kids gravitated to, and we loved it. This was how Sergio and I organically discovered how to raise our family. We wanted Carla and Sam to feel comfortable bringing their friends home, at a place where they could have gatherings and parties in a safe and secure environment. For what it's worth, I still struggle to understand the difference between a 'gathering' and a 'party', but both kids assured me that it had something to do with the overall numbers attending and how pre-planned the event was!

I mention our party house now because our last stop was Amsterdam, and I fell in love with this gorgeous snow-covered city on my first glance from the train carriage. We had a fantastic 'crooked house' booked on Airbnb, which would accommodate me in the attic in my king-size bed and provide heaps of room for Carla and Paul downstairs in the lounge room, on the two big couches.

Now, I know the world is a very big place, but it was ridiculously amazing how many local friends from Melbourne both Carla and Paul knew in Amsterdam at that time. Of the seven nights we stayed in that wonderful old house, we had three fantastic evenings hosting dinner parties with young Aussie friends. They would cycle over in the snow to join us, and some would also crash on the huge couches for the night. It was like a version of old times in Flemington, with lots of great food, wine, beer and laughter. Home truly is where the heart is. It's not about your favourite possessions or collectables, it's only ever really about people.

I learnt a lot that week about the resilience of young people, and the unbridled zest they all have for life and all that it offers. I honestly don't believe I could have endured living on the other side of the world at such a young age, and be prepared to bicycle around in the snow and freezing temperatures and live in tiny, cramped quarters miles away from where they usually socialised. I know for a fact I could have never done this, and it's no accident that all of our young Aussie visitors have grown into wonderful, fully fledged adults with so much to offer each other and society in general.

Aside from the fun of being away with Carla, the knowledge that my family would never be whole and complete again was never far from the forefront of my mind. The day finally arrived when Carla and I had to say our very sad farewells at Amsterdam airport, and I began my long journey home alone.

Most of January had already passed us by, and there was still so much to do before our big house move. The pre-planned garage sale was thankfully a huge success, and we were lucky enough to have the space and the privacy of holding it in the old stable area, which was our family room. It was also an added bonus that a civilised starting time was adhered to, because no one could gain access until the big stable doors were swung open on sale day. Mind you, there was a considerable queue waiting when the doors opened at 9.00 am on the Saturday.

Much of the furniture not going to Fitzroy North, which just so happened to be the bulk of it, was unexpectedly sold the day before the garage sale to old neighbourhood friends of ours, Helene and Jim. It pleased Sergio and I greatly to know that a big part of our Farnham Street home would remain intact, just at another location. Our nature strip on the street also became a terrific resting place for any goods too nice to ditch but not quite appealing enough to sell, and these pieces went to whoever drove past and stopped to collect them. At times there was quite a flurry happening out front, but it gave us a huge amount of pleasure to know that our old possessions were finding good homes.

Moving day finally arrived and it was relatively painless, due to the fact that so many boxes of our crockery, glassware, clothing, bedding and so on had already been moved into our new home by us a few days beforehand, after the property settlement in Fitzroy North had taken place. One smallish moving van did the trick and we were all moved in as planned, in mid-February 2013.

Jingles and Megan were the last treasures to leave Farnham Street, and surprisingly they moved in without much ado at all. Just like in Amsterdam, where I was so very aware that it is the people who make a home, Jingles and Megan obviously felt the same way, because they settled in immediately simply because Sergio and I were there. It had now been just over nine months since Sam's accident.

Paul, Milly, me and Carla in Amsterdam, January 2013

CHAPTER 12

Signs and messages

At some stage in 2012, post 3 May, I asked Carla to help me establish a Facebook account so I too could keep in touch with existing family and friends, just as the rest of the world already seemed to be doing very well and had done so for some time. I was a very late starter into the unknown mysteries of cyber chat and online communication. I had mastered email and calendar invites, but that was the full extent of my computer expertise. I saw first hand, via Carla's Facebook connections, how instantly you could receive words of comfort and affection from those who could not be there in person, or who were just wanting to remain in very regular if not daily contact.

My standstill start as a Facebooker took off immediately, and before I knew it I was reconnecting far and wide with long-lost friends, many of them from my own days at Tatura Kindergarten, Tatura Primary School and of course Mooroopna High School. I certainly don't wish to alienate anyone at all, but one new connection in particular was a real life changer for me.

I received a friend request from a woman called Sandra Uzowuru (nee Newton), an old kinder and primary school friend from 1964 to 1971. We would often sleep over at one another's homes, and I always had very fond memories of staying many times out on the sheep farm in Dhurringile with the Newton family.

It was here I had learnt how to catch yabbies by tying small cubes of fresh meat to a length of string and dangling it into the dam or irrigation channel. Unknowing freshwater crustaceans would march up the string and into the obligatory plastic bucket that was also required in this high-tech fishing exercise, and it would soon be brimming with live yabbies. We would hightail it back home, and our catch would be boiled and served with vinegar and salt and be enjoyed by all six Newtons and myself.

As so often happens in life, Sandra and I went our separate ways after finishing primary school. During secondary school, we sadly had absolutely no contact whatsoever. This is not at all unusual, albeit disappointing. There is a very special reason for singling Sandra out, and it really does need further explanation.

Sandra had survived a near-death experience in a horrific fire while on a school camp from Shepparton South Technical School, when she was only twelve years old. I can still remember seeing this on the local TV news at the time, and not surprisingly this dreadful experience changed Sandra's own life forever. Two girls sleeping close by did not survive, one of them sleeping in the bed that had originally been allocated to Sandra.

I noticed on Sandra's Facebook blurb that she had been living in Sydney for many years, and was studying mediumship via correspondence with a world-renowned English medium based in the United States called Lisa Williams. She was also apparently taking further tuition with a Sydney-based medium called Florence King. I was clueless at that stage about who Lisa Williams or Florence King were, but it was not lost on me that something as obscure and non-mainstream as mediumship could be somehow studied. I was very curious indeed.

It took Sandra a little while to make direct contact with me, partly due to her own amazement and bewilderment as to what was happening to her, but mostly because she did not want to upset Sergio, Carla or me. Sandra was starting to receive little messages from an unknown 'source', and yet she instinctively knew these communications were from Sam, our Sam!

Sandra eventually shared these messages with me, just as they came to her. Nothing was filtered, she just gave whatever she was given. Sam provided her with information about many random things that made total sense to me, such as the bubble baths he had daily as a little boy and how I had let all of my newly purchased flowering pots die on our new balcony. I was gobsmacked reading Sandra's email as I rode the tram into the city, to start yet another day of work at Amigos.

I just wish I hadn't started reading the very beautifully worded email on public transport, as it was an extremely emotional experience. Both Sam and Carla had bubble baths for years in the big spa bath at Farnham Street and both loved them. Reading Sam saying 'Bubbles, Mummy, more bubbles' certainly had my attention, as he would say exactly this.

When Sandra pointed out Sam's disappointment that I had killed all the brand new seedlings in the summer heat in the first week of moving in (which I shamefully had done), I could not ignore what was being said. According to Sandra, Sam wanted me to go and sit on the park bench opposite our new home to talk to him. He would be there, and I would feel his presence. Sandra also went on to say many other amazing things, one of them being that Sam wanted Sergio to get on his bike and feel the wind in his hair and to start laughing again, as Sam missed hearing his dad laugh!

A few things need to be pointed out here. First, Sandra lived in Sydney and had never been to or even seen our new home, or the old one for that matter. Second, I had not posted any photos of my shrivelled plants on Facebook (although I did later on for Sandra's benefit). Sandra had no way of knowing I had killed every new seedling due to a lack of water and care. Third, she had no idea we did actually have a park bench opposite that looked directly into our place. Last, she did not know that Sergio was an avid cyclist who did usually gain much pleasure from feeling the wind in his hair while enjoying his two-wheeled pursuit. Not surprisingly, laughter was probably not as forthcoming and as regular as it used to be with Sergio, and I can absolutely understand Sam expressing this through Sandra.

I felt compelled to do as Sam asked of me via Sandra, and I did go and sit on that park bench looking back to our new home. I allowed myself to just 'be'. I did feel Sam's presence, as I had been feeling it all along, but somehow having this insight from Sandra made it all the more real and powerful for me.

I sat, Sam 'talked', and I listened. It was tearful, cathartic and slightly weird all at once, and I did go straight from the park bench on foot to the local plant nursery nearby to buy a new selection of seedlings and potted colour. I took photos of the before and after gardening disaster and triumph, and I know Sandra was thrilled by what she had just achieved as a relative newcomer to mediumship.

When Sandra first mentioned that Sam was also sending us messages by leaving small white feathers, I was actually a little sceptical; it was all sounding too generic and whimsical. I preferred the more specific messages about dead plants, the need to laugh while bike riding and park bench chats. I certainly wasn't doubting Sandra at all, it just seemed a bit too airy fairy. I can't honestly remember when I saw my first little white feather, but I do know it came at a time when I needed such a sign, and it lifted my heart more than I can describe.

After this, I would ask Sam to send me a little feather to let me know that he was hearing my messages to him. I didn't request this of him every day, but when I did I started to find little white feathers on the left-hand side, almost at the top of the stairs at Amigos. This spot was just near where I stood each day to welcome guests to our restaurant. I never removed them. I left that for the overnight cleaner, as those feathers made me smile whenever I walked past them, which was very often as I went up and down the stairs many times at every meal service.

On the day that would have been Sam's twenty-first birthday there were three little white feathers all grouped together in a triangle, one for each of us. It was a beautiful gift from Sam to acknowledge his birthday. It wasn't long afterwards that we started finding small white feathers inside at home, but only on special occasions such as birthdays and anniversaries. It was amazing and so beautiful. The feathers would be carefully placed on Sergio's desk, or by either side of our bed, or in a doorway, where they wouldn't be easily missed. It's important to mention that we don't have any feather bedding at all, and many of these feathers appeared during the winter months when all of the windows and doors were firmly shut.

Just prior to Christmas in 2015, Sergio, Carla and I decided to finally go to a stunning place called Montsalvat, which has been an artists' colony since 1934 and was in the leafy northern suburb of Eltham, in Melbourne. It had been on our radar for ages as a lovely place to visit, have lunch and stroll through the French provincial-inspired gardens and buildings.

Finally we made it there, and on arrival we went into the large public gallery to see the work of the two international artists who were the main drawcard of the exhibition. As I often did, and still do, I felt Sam's presence there as we wandered around taking in the varying painting styles of the two artists. Since we were already there, it made sense to buy tickets to allow us to venture through the beautiful grounds that we had heard so much about. I went to the counter to pay for the tickets, and although I only asked for three I was given four. When I gave one back, the girl behind the desk said she thought there were four of us. She was spot on, but I couldn't really say as much!

Prior to our garden walk, we had lunch in the restaurant area next to the main gallery. A small and quaint rustic room was attached that was housing a relatively moderate exhibition by a local artist, Claire

McCall. I was not familiar with her colourful and creative oils, mainly of children depicted in seaside scenes, but I loved what I saw of them on a quick visit to the bathroom.

As I left this small showing, I noticed a beautiful painting beside the door that went outside to the bathroom. It was of a young girl and little boy playing in the beach shallows and building sand castles. It immediately made me think of both Carla and Sam in their younger years, and the boy in particular even looked a bit like Sam.

I mentioned this to Sergio and Carla when I sat back at our lunch table, then they both made subsequent trips past the paintings on the way to the loo. Sergio obviously looked at more of the artwork than I had, and he commented on a painting in the far corner that looked exactly like Sam as a young boy. The boy was playing in the water, and was even wearing the same dual-coloured sun protection top that Sam had when he was about five or six years old.

Of course, Carla and I both wanted to see this painting for ourselves, and we all stood there stunned by the painted likeness to Sam. It was as if we had commissioned the painting to be done from an old photograph. We immediately decided to buy this beautiful piece, and when we happened to look below the painting, there on the floor was a little white feather.

What more could we ask for? We found Claire, the artist, who fortuitously happened to be there that day, and we bought the painting from her on the spot. I just wish I had had the foresight to ask her who the little boy in the painting was. It was probably best, though, that I hadn't, for in my mind it is our Sam. Everyone who knew Sam and sees the painting also assumes that it is him.

I cautiously started sharing my feather stories with close friends, including some of Sam's mates. Most looked quite sceptical about the possibilities of Sam being able to send small feathers, or anything else for that matter, and I always understood their reluctance to embrace the possibility.

One night about a year ago the three of us had a beautiful barbeque dinner at the home of Jo and Sam, a gorgeous mother and son who we have known for years from Wesley College days. Jo is extremely open minded to any and all possibilities when it comes to dealing with spirit, and all things of a psychic nature. Understandably, it's fair to say that her Sam was not buying into this weird conversation about spirits and signs. We had such a fun night; it was great to catch up again and also to see their new home for the first time.

Even though it was a barbeque dinner, we sat inside at the dining room table to enjoy the lovely meal that was served. We talked a lot about our Sam, as we always did with those who knew and loved him.

We shared much laughter and possibly a few tears, as both of these emotions now seemed to come concurrently for me. The next day I received a very excited text message and photo from Sam (Gussy), showing a photograph of a small white feather resting on one of the dining room chairs; it had been discovered after we left. How absolutely fantastic for all of us.

Caulfield, me and Charlie at one of Sam's birthday parties

Sam, Christine and me in Italy, 2010

Dinner at Azza's in Sam's honour

CHAPTER 13

Graffiti tags and stories

It was the day of Sam's memorial service that I discovered our son had a love for something both Sergio and I hated: graffiti! From among all of Sam's nicknames – Sammy, Da Vinci, SOS, Sam A – there was also Clerk and Clerks. I was very familiar with all the others but not Clerk or Clerks, or even the grandiose title of King Clerk. Who was this person, and why so mysterious? I had come across random spray cans at home in the past and had naively hoped they were for some school art project, or something else just as remotely feasible.

It became very apparent over beers with some of Sam's mates after his passing that Sam was a prolific 'tagger', signing the moniker of Clerks, Clerk or King Clerk whenever and wherever he could.

At first I was really annoyed and even angry that Sam could do such a thing. We, like most parents, hated the senseless act of scribbling your alias on all manner of surfaces in the name of graffiti, art or tagging. It was to us a mindless act of vandalism and it was nothing to be proud of. Then another incredibly strange number of things started to become clear to us, as bit by bit we began noticing the signs.

After moving to Fitzroy North, I started going back through the many boxes of articles, letters, cards, photographs and so on relating to Sam's accident, and I vividly remember looking at one of the newspaper photographs in *The Age* newspaper taken immediately after the accident on Westgarth Street in Northcote.

Our car was in the photograph, with a tarpaulin tossed over it. The 'sign' was missed in an earlier photograph, from a different newspaper, because of the angle of the shot. In this photo, you could clearly see that a power pole had been tagged directly behind where all three boys had passed away, and the signature on it was 'Clerk'. Some time previously, Sam had signed his tag name on the very pole next to where he, Raph and Jesse left this earth. It was unbelievable, and yet there it was.

On my first day catching the number eleven tram into work from our new tram stop, which is only metres away from our home, I happened to look down at the base of a light pole just as my tram was pulling up. Here, for all to see, was another piece of sideways painted graffiti, and the signature belonged to none other than 'Clerks'! Sam had somehow, in advance, tagged the very place where his family would stand to catch a tram into the city. Catching public transport was something we did often, so we were sure to see it at some stage. Absolutely unbelievable!

To me these signs were so wonderful, so full of hope and so much more. I have always been a person who believes that everything happens for a reason, and once again this was proven to be correct. On a hot summer's night, not that long after moving into Fitzroy North, we were having drinks with friends on the balcony when we heard our names being called from the park opposite. It turned out to be one of Sam's best mates, Caulfield, from Wesley College, and also one of his travelling companions on the Thailand trip taken just before the accident.

Caulfield came up and joined us for a beer. He sat for some time in a strange state of animated shock, as he expressed his disbelief that Sergio and I had bought this very townhouse, in this very spot, when we could have moved to any suburb or street anywhere in Melbourne. We really weren't sure where all of this was leading, but eventually he managed to tell us that one night Sam, Raph and himself decided to tag the framework and fabric screenings of an entire building site, which it turned out was now our new address!

I am not condoning for a second what they did, but it is also not lost on us that Sam, Raph and Caulfield had graffitied the 'bones' of what was to become our future home. Please forgive me if I say this made me feel way more amazed and happy than it did angry.

Azza, me, Yano and Sergio at Sam's 25th birthday party, 2018

Kevin, Morris, Jeremy and Kai at Sam's 25th birthday at Cafe Trutrack, 2018

CHAPTER 14

Sitting in circle

Almost a year somehow came and went, and by now Carla was well and truly back from her European stay with Paul. They were renting a house back in our old neighbourhood of Flemington. She had recommenced university and was finishing her public relations course at RMIT, and also working madly in the box office at Dracula's theatre restaurant to subsidise her living costs.

By this stage we had settled in very happily at Alfred Crescent, and we tried as best we could to keep going on in a positive way in our respective lives. Without a doubt the change of suburbs and downsizing from our large family home to a comparatively smaller townhouse that better suited our needs had helped us with our forced living adjustment. I am so pleased I listened to my inner voice and not that of the masses, who consider it a poor decision to make huge changes too rapidly.

I firmly believe you should abide by your heart and own gut feel and make a call from there. The generic standards meant little to me, and I am happy we have continued to do things in our own way, and in a way that makes sense to us.

Since making our move to our new home, I have continued to read many, many books from that previously unknown and mysterious aisle found in all bookshops. I was incredibly curious about wanting to know all about mysterious topics such as light workers, past life regression, mediumship, psychic development, psychic sciences, angels, guides and a whole host of other alien and previously unexplored things.

On a whim, Sergio and I decided to take our first-ever cruise to the Pacific region, leaving on Australia Day in January 2014. It was just for ten days, the plan being to totally relax and unwind. We flew up to Sydney, and after collecting our luggage joined a rather large group of holidaymakers who were all standing in the P&O Cruises queue, waiting to catch multiple buses to where our ship would be departing.

This was all new to us and very exciting at the same time. We cleared customs, and parted with our luggage just as you do when flying internationally from the airport. We duly sailed out beneath Sydney Harbour Bridge, with music blaring and the loud ship horn joining in the chorus. It was a real carnival atmosphere and we felt terrific about whatever was to unfold. Sergio and I had booked an outside cabin, high up on the ship and with a balcony. It was fabulous and so therapeutic for us and our souls.

It actually was the perfect trip at that particular time in our lives, because just prior to leaving I had been feeling extremely restless and in need of some sort of self-help, guidance, therapy, personal assistance, psychological intervention, God knows what really, but I absolutely needed something.

Again I resorted to Google, which had rarely ever let me down in the past, and I found the name of Toni Reilly, a random woman who was running a newly formed group or, for want of another word, a circle. As with Lorraine Culross, the first medium we consulted, I just went with my gut feeling and booked myself into the first eight-week session, a complete term. Unfortunately, because of the cruise dates I missed the first week, but from then on I rarely missed any opportunity to sit in circle.

Circle was a totally new experience for me. I arrived at the appointed time and entered the healing centre in the suburb of St Kilda, where Toni rented a room for her hour and a half long group sessions. We had been asked to bring along a journal so we could record our experiences after meditating, and I still find it totally amazing to re-read the words I penned each week immediately afterwards.

There always seemed to be varying numbers of attendees each week, always women. Toni was a delight, and I felt so comfortable with her from the very beginning. As I soon discovered, she was also a wonderful and gifted medium and psychic. At the start of each session we would all meditate, another new experience for me, but I took to it instantly and then realised I had been inadvertently meditating all my life, in what I thought was just very animated and informative daydreaming. I felt utterly at home and absolutely where I needed to be at this time in my life.

My weekly circle group became both my healing and therapy group all rolled into one. I cried every single week with a bunch of complete strangers who knew nothing about me initially, but they were all so totally supportive and genuinely kind and caring. I found myself talking about Sam, about us, about all sorts of things, and it was therapeutic and cathartic in every aspect. When we meditated, I started to see Sam and my other loved ones. I could hear their words, feel their love and their very presence; it was amazing. More tears!

As my journal started to fill, so did my mind: I needed to delve deeper into what we were learning. I loved being able to immediately and intuitively read tarot cards for the other girls, and learn later that my findings were very accurate. I had never even seen tarot or any types of spiritual cards before, but it didn't take long for me to buy my own pack of Rider-Waite tarot cards. The cards seemed to somehow 'speak' to me and the information they gave was absolutely astonishing, certainly for me and also very often for whoever I was giving a reading.

During meditation and afterwards, I could feel the change of energy within the room and within the others present. I would receive the most amazing guidance when I meditated and I was able to be fully immersed in my meditative state, so that I felt I no longer had a physical body.

I have kept all of the journals filled with my meditations, and I often re-read them and wonder who in the hell actually wrote that! The answer of course is always the same: it was, in fact, me. I am still always astonished at what I would see, hear and feel during these times in a naturally altered state of mind.

I would like to now share one very emotive experience with you, which came about after I meditated at a circle session in January 2016. I had set the intention of being shown my very own garden of life, and I was not disappointed!

I was flying over a beautiful field that was coloured in every shade of pink and green, and also every other colour imaginable.

I asked to see my own plot in this gorgeous garden of life, and I was taken to a garden bed that was planted beside a lovely stately tree.

Two of the flowers in my plot needed propping up. These were my mum and step-dad Bill, as they were getting older now and just needed some extra help to stand upright.

Some flowers were dead. These represented Sam, Dad and my grandparents, and I was to take these dead flowers and keep them close to my heart always.

Other flowers were yet to break through the earth properly from within the ground. They were still bulbs, and were people that I was yet to meet in my life.

Sunflowers stood tall, proud and strong; these were my family and lifelong friends.

More flowers were very small and these friendships were still growing and blossoming.

There were small patches of soil where nothing grew. This was where past friends who were no longer in my life once stood. When these flowers died they simply blew away in the wind.

I then flew over this massive garden and I could see all of the other plots. Some were just rabbit burrows with nothing growing and others had only one or two flowers standing brightly. Others were full, brimming and lovely. These plots depicted the gardens of life of unknown and unseen people within our realm.

It was the most wondrous and thought-provoking of meditations I had experienced at that stage. Such a simple analogy of life, my life: it was clear and concise and made perfect and total sense to me. Now whenever I want answers to questions, or to gain insight into certain situations, I sit quietly and meditate and the answers just come.

Through the wonders of this altered state of mind I am also able to be with Sam, Dad and all of the spirits who have gone before me, and I feel that it's my way to visit with them, just as they return the favour and make their presence known to me in my dreams.

Because of Toni's other work commitments as the owner and facilitator of SoulLife, a training facility for personal transformation, our circle group was taken over by another beautiful woman and equally gifted medium called Kristen Hill. My own personal growth and confidence continued to grow in what I was learning and experiencing. When time permitted I would re-read my many, many journal entries, and I was still always amazed by what I had written after coming out of my insightful meditations.

Somehow as a person I was feeling stronger, wiser and far more confident in what I was learning, doing and experiencing, and most importantly I was finally feeling that a healing process was starting within me and it was working.

Sam was present at each and every circle meeting. I felt his presence, as did some of the other women, who were also on a path to advance and explore their own spiritual side. He truly helped one lovely woman, Ruth, to feel more confident in developing her own gift of mediumship. Ruth was able to accurately describe what Sam looked like, his build, his colouring, his stunning eyes, right down to his gorgeous lopsided smile. Ruth had never seen a picture of Sam; he just went to her and thus became the first spirit Ruth had ever properly 'seen'. It was such a beautiful moment to share with her and I was so very proud of our boy.

Kristen had also never seen a photo of Sam or of where we lived, and yet she was able to share the most wonderful information with me.

On the day before circle one week Kristen had felt Sam come to her during the day, and she took me aside the next night to share what had happened. She had seen Sam reclining on our couch at home wearing a pair of boxer shorts and a tee shirt, his standard 'uniform' at Farnham Street when we didn't have visitors. Kristen said that Sam was trying to get the cat's attention on the end of the couch. This was incredible as Megan, Carla's cat, had a permanent bed on the L-shaped return of the couch. She did in fact live right there.

Remember when I mentioned the importance of the movie *Ghost* earlier? There is a scene where Patrick Swayze's character, called Sam – yes, Sam! – is madly trying to get their cat's attention to alert his girlfriend Molly, played by Demi Moore, that there was an intruder in their apartment. He managed to send the cat into a noisy hissy fit and the burglar escaped, but without hurting Molly or being seen by her.

Kristen had me fascinated about our Sam and our cat, because Megan would often start to call out frantically in the middle of the night and run around the furniture wailing crazily. This would only last for a few seconds, then she would settle back down and go back to sleep. I now had Kristen's full attention, and she asked me to check the clock next time this happened to see if the time meant anything special to me.

That night, almost as if on cue, Megan started her raucous calling and racing around the lounge room. I went straight into our bathroom to check the time on the digital clock: it was 3.05 am. Sam passed away on the third day of the fifth month, 3 May.

Megan continues to rip around the furniture, calling out excitedly, a few times a week, although not always at 3.05 am. I do know that it is

Sam who firmly has her attention and I lay in bed and absolutely love knowing this.

I still sit in circle most weeks, but now in Elwood with another wonderful medium called Tina Orfanos. I thoroughly enjoy being taught new aspects of mediumship and psychic practices, and there has rarely been a session in which I have not learnt something new or grown a little bit more as a person.

Some mediums just know from birth they have the gift of mediumship, and they organically learn to develop their skills over time for themselves. This is not always the case, just as it wasn't for me. I had to have a major tragedy happen in my life before I made my wonderful discovery. It truly is a bittersweet outcome.

I recall asking Toni Reilly where she did her training as a medium, and she said three words that have altered the course of my life forever after: Arthur Findlay College.

CHAPTER 15

My turning point

I am not someone who finds it difficult to make a quick decision about most things in life, whether it be trying something new, changing job roles, joining random groups or travelling to unknown places. From the moment Toni told me she had attended the Arthur Findlay College of Psychic Sciences in England to learn more about her mediumship development, I could think of not much else.

In typical fashion my mind was already made up, and by early May 2014 I had booked myself and my old childhood friend, Sandra Uzowuru, into two back-to-back six and seven day courses, commencing in February 2015.

As you know, Sandra and I had reconnected via Facebook after decades of separation, with no contact whatsoever. It was thanks to Facebook that we became very much aware we were both on a similar journey in wanting to develop properly as psychic mediums.

There was one small issue: the fact that Sandra and I had actually not seen one another since 1971. Despite this, we booked to go away together for a quick Thomas Cook tour of London, Oxford, Cambridge and Dubai on the way home. We were also to spend thirteen nights together sharing a bedroom at a training college for mediums in the lovely Essex countryside. It certainly was not your mainstream holiday abroad that is readily advertised at your local Flight Centre.

Initially, Carla and Sergio were a tad concerned about how well this would all pan out, as Sandra and I had parted as twelve year olds and were teaming up for a fairly lengthy overseas adventure some forty-three years later. Point taken! Fortunately, Sandra had a catch-up reunion organised in Melbourne, with old workmates from her days working at ICI, in September 2014. It was decided that dining at Amigos with her girlfriends made perfect sense, and in that way I could join them straight afterwards at 9.00 pm when my maître d' hosting shift was finished.

Sandra and her old work friends arrived and I was busting to sit down with them, but that would still have to wait a good two hours. As soon as I was able, I joined their table and met Sandra's friends. Those poor ladies had no chance in the world of getting a word in, as Sandra and I were in full flight talking about our upcoming UK trip, our mediumship, Sam, our families and pretty much everything else that had taken place in the missing forty-three years since we had last seen one another!

Sandra had been overseas a few times previously, but never to the UK. It was a country she had always wanted to visit and now she was going. I was lucky enough to have been a few times beforehand and I always loved going back to where my own family origins lay, albeit about four generations ago.

Because we were travelling so far, it made perfect sense to start the trip a little earlier and to stay on a little longer at the finish. I had promised that I would visit two lovely old girlfriends from my high school days at Mooroopna: Helen and her husband David, from Standlake near Oxford, and also Lorraine and her husband Graham in Dubai on our way home. It was also decided that we would stay in Cambridge with Seb and his mum, Brigitte, for two nights. Sandra was most welcomed by everyone to join the party, and all of the arrangements were duly made.

I flew to Sydney and met Sandra's lovely family, her husband, Emmanuel, and daughter, Mollie, and our journey began in full. We intentionally left the day after Sergio's Valentine's Day birthday, departing on 15 February and scheduled to return home on 12 March, the day before what would have been Sam's twenty-second birthday on 13 March. The way the course dates and birthdays all lined up was hard to ignore; it was absolutely 'meant to be'.

And so began an amazing trip that was never without signs, signals and evidence that Sam was most certainly with us. A boutique hotel had been booked for two nights in Paddington, in order to place us very central to most things. The collection of gorgeous old Georgian homes, all linked together, that formed our hotel was the perfect way to start feeling that we were very much in London town. We had booked twin beds in the same room, but with many English hotels never being overly generous size wise we were practically sharing a large bed, separated only by some sheets and blankets down the middle.

On arrival into our room, I put my black leather handbag down onto the crisp white doona cover, and before my eyes I saw a tiny white feather appear out of nowhere, about eight inches above my bag. It fluttered gently down and landed on the bag. I was speechless, and thankfully Sandra just happened to look in my direction and also at my handbag at that very moment. It was she that dropped the F bomb this time! We had arrived, and so too had Sam: how absolutely brilliant.

I had such a wonderful and constant feeling that Sam was with us on this trip. I knew within myself that he approved wholeheartedly of what we were both doing, and I couldn't wait to see what he had in mind for us when we reached the college in Essex six days later.

It was wonderful being with both Helen and David, after so many years of not keeping in touch. It is true, that it really is possible to pick up old friendships where they left off, and this certainly occurred here. Sandra just so happened to have grown up in the same rural farming area as Helen, a tiny place called Dhurringile, famous for the prison farm located there and not much else. It became all the more apparent that we, as people, are all so intertwined in one way or another. Even Sergio and David had been friends during the 1970s and 1980s, but they had not seen one another since.

During the daylight hours, we girls would drive around this stunning area with Helen at the wheel, visiting Oxford, the Cotswolds, Blenheim Palace and a variety of ancient pubs and tearooms, and without fail we would come across little white feathers in our travels. I would always say to Helen and Sandra: 'Look, there's one for each of us', as they were often in batches of three. It was mid-winter, it was cold, wet and bird free, and yet the feathers were always there. Helen was now on feather watch as well, and it brought much pleasure to all of us when the feathers regularly appeared.

David cooked the most amazing dinners, which were ready on our return to Standlake; we all shared this beautiful food, wine and never-ending conversation. It was the perfect way to ease ourselves into our English holiday and study trip. Both Helen and David were very supportive with regard to what we were studying, which was wonderful because it can certainly be quite daunting and religiously confusing or even offensive to some.

Matt, me and Seb in the UK, 2015

The beautiful city of Cambridge, staying with Seb and Brigitte, was our next stop for two terrific nights, and it was great to be able to see them both again. It had been two years since our first catch up in

Brussels, Belgium, when I visited in 2013 with Carla. John, Brigitte's partner from London, and my other surrogate son, Matt, surprised me by arriving from London to join in the celebrations. We had an absolute ball, going to ancient pubs and having a home-cooked feast at Brigitte's home. They are such fantastic memories to hold dear, which I certainly do, and I'm sure that Sandra does as well.

At last the time had come, and after an hour-long bus trip we were finally almost at Arthur Findlay College to commence our tuition on the Sunday afternoon. We were dropped off at the National Express bus terminal, at busy Stansted Airport, and it was then a reasonably quick taxi ride from there to Stansted Hall, as the building at the college is called. It is impossible to describe our excitement as we were driven up the lengthy driveway to the three-storey red brick Victorian mansion that had been a world-renowned teaching college for mediums for fifty-one years.

Arthur Findlay College, Essex, UK

Our twin bedroom was located somewhere in that stunning maze of a building, which houses ninety students plus all of the incredible tutors who teach there under the one roof. The tutors are there by invitation only, and it is a huge honour to be asked to teach at the college. They come from many countries worldwide, as do the students.

After unpacking and hanging our clothes in the wardrobe, we were ready to join everyone for coffee and the welcome address, followed by dinner. At 7.30 pm we attended our first ever spiritualist church service, which was being held in the sanctuary, originally the old orangery in this vast mansion.

I won't go into too much detail here, but the Spiritualists' National Union was bequeathed this stately dwelling, Stansted Hall, in 1964 by the late Arthur Findlay and his wife, with the strict understanding that it would be used as a teaching facility for the advancement of psychic sciences and the teaching of mediumship.

Arthur Findlay was not a medium himself. In fact, he was initially sceptical of such practices, until he attended a séance and witnessed with his own eyes that contact could indeed be made between the two worlds. He soon became an advocate of spiritualism and his legacy was to leave Stansted Hall to all future generations of mediums, to enable them to have a place in which the finest tutors from all around the world could assist them in honing their skills. Being Kerry, from Tatura, and Sandra, from Dhurringile in rural Australia, was somewhat confronting in such surroundings.

During the church service on the Sunday night I witnessed my first mediumship demonstration. The demonstration was absolutely amazing, and the church service was both uplifting and enjoyable. Unlike all other church services that I had previously attended (which, I should add, were low in number), I thoroughly loved the inclusion of contemporary music and relevant, thought-provoking addresses, which made total sense in today's modern world.

The people conducting the service were all tutors under whom we would be training in the coming week, and at least one of them was an ordained minister of the spiritualist church. Spiritualists believe primarily in the survival of spirit after death, and their key objective is to provide evidence of survival via mediumship. That's it in a nutshell!

We could see that two of the tutors were not taking any active part in the service, but were sitting quietly and meditating. When they respectively took their turns to do a mediumship demonstration the service went to another level, which until then I had never experienced.

To say it was totally incredible and amazing does not do the demonstration justice. Correct Christian and sometimes surnames were voiced, the manner of passing was shared, physical likenesses were described, hobbies and passions from this lifetime were mentioned and information was given about what was happening in the recipients' lives here on earth. Evidence of survival into the afterlife was the aim, and from what I was seeing and hearing it was certainly given. Sandra and I could not wait to start classes the following morning.

I initially chose our two courses quite randomly, based on a few things that fitted my needs. First, they had to be early in the year, as I could not wait any longer to start my tuition, and second, the courses could not fall on either Sergio's or Sam's birthdays, as I wanted Sergio, Carla and me to all be together for those celebrations. After more googling, two courses jumped off the page at me and that's what we signed up for. Week one was 'Journey of the Soul', a mixture of mediumship and philosophy for mixed levels, followed by 'The Power

Within', which was all about mediumship, also for all levels of ability. It was excellent news for me, as I was very much a beginner at this stage.

Just like at circle, I always preferred to not give away anything about myself and certainly not any information about Sam and how he passed. I wanted any enlightenment to come from the other side via the mediums, so then I would know that only Sam, Dad or another of my loved ones was providing the evidence. Sandra and I both agreed that neither of us would share our stories with anyone, we would just wait to see what unfolded.

Our group of twenty-eight studying 'Journey of the Soul' was broken into two smaller groups, those who were very experienced mediums and people like us. All of the other sixty or so students at the college that week were studying other courses in different classrooms.

I vividly remember crying my way through much of that first week, but it was actually an amazingly cleansing and cathartic time for me. I needed to experience everything I was going through to prepare myself for the massive change that was taking place in my life and also, essentially, in me. Whether I knew it or not, I was at a point of no return and I was thrilled about it. This was where I was meant to be, and I embraced every single aspect of it.

We started every class with a beautiful and enlightening meditation, to set us up for the long days, with the first class starting at 9.30 am and the last one finishing at 9.00 pm. Everyone was grateful that the bar opened for two hours each night, until 11.00 pm, then it was off to bed for some solid sleep before arriving at breakfast the next morning at 8.00 am.

One morning early on in the week, as I dressed for breakfast, I found a small white feather stuck to my sleeve as I put on a new outfit from the wardrobe. How wonderful this made me feel, that Sam was just letting me know in no uncertain terms he was very much with me. I also believe he was acknowledging that he was happy to be witnessing what I was doing.

During that first week at college, I had a number of feathers come my way. Another tiny white plume appeared a few days later, stuck on a different jacket that came straight from the closed wardrobe in the bedroom with the shut windows, which was also devoid of any down bedding!

We were incredibly fortunate to experience so many unbelievable things that week, and on our second day I clearly recall that a couple of the well-seasoned mediums from the advanced class were going to do some spontaneous readings for us all, as a group, after dinner. A lovely and very experienced medium, an Englishwoman called Val, stood and took her place in the centre of the largish circle in the gorgeous old library, which was still brimming with Arthur Findlay's massive collection of ancient books.

I immediately felt Sam's presence on my left-hand side, which is where he always seems to go. He is never on my right-hand side, as this is where I feel my dad's presence. My left lower leg is always freezing when Sam is present, and I can always feel the change in the energy around me. Val knew absolutely nothing about me other than I was from Australia, something that is hard to disguise, no matter how multicultural the group.

Val said she had a young male spirit with her and then looked directly at me and said, I believe it is your son. Thankfully Sandra took my hand and I tried to stay strong and composed enough to hear what Sam had to say via Val. She said that Sam was a very positive and spiritual person, mentioning a folder of photographs showing family and friends and how all who have one cherish it. (I believe she was referring to the folded cardboard handout from Sam's memorial service, which could stand up. It comprised only favourite photographs and no words, other than Sam's name and his dates of birth and passing.)

She mentioned Thailand and his love of that country and their culture. She went on to say that Sam was very proud of me for what I was doing to learn about the survival of spirit and mediumship: she said he knew exactly what was going on. Val talked about the very real and strong connection Sam and me have with one another. March was a very significant month for Sam, something to celebrate: it is the month of his birthday. Val was shown a small young woman who is still really hurting (I believe that this was Carla). In closing, Val said it was a very sudden passing and that Sam's eyes were so lovely and striking, as was his smile.

Needless to say I was both very emotional and also flying on cloud nine. I actually had one of the memorial cards with me, which I silently kissed each night before bed and again in the morning when Sandra was not looking. I wanted to take it to show Val at breakfast time so she could see what Sam looked like, as she had described him so well and had most importantly captured the beautiful feel of him. As I took the card out of my leather folder, I realised I had inadvertently put a second one in there, so now I could give Val her own copy. Nothing is an accident: I had somehow done that unknowingly for this very reason.

At the beginning of the week we had been told that thirty minute one-on-one readings would be available to book with our tutors over the duration of the week. I could not make a booking quickly enough. I managed to have my reading with the wonderful and gifted Janet Parker, on 27 February 2015, and it was forty-five pounds very well spent.

Prior to the reading I asked Sam to be there for me, and I put in a special request that he talk about all of the feathers I had received personally, and also about the ones we had seen during the previous week with both Helen and Sandra.

Much amazing evidence was received at the reading given by Janet, but I was especially blown away when Sam kept interrupting what Janet was saying with the words 'They're just for you, they're just for you'. At first, neither of us knew what Sam meant by this. It was only when I told Janet about the feathers we had seen and received, and how I kept saying to Helen and Sandra that Sam was sharing them with us all. Apparently he wasn't, and this was his way of talking about the feathers just as I had asked him to do. They were just for me: Sam's very special and beautiful gift. Janet and I were both thrilled.

Unfortunately, our first course had to come to an end after breakfast on the Saturday, and we both farewelled our newfound friends as they all departed to various corners of the world. Sandra and I had a free day to explore the nearby village of Stansted Mountfitchet, only a few kilometres walk from the college. We rugged up in our thick coats, donned scarfs and boots and off we set along the lovely old unmade laneway that passed by the private fishing club and the horse paddocks on the way to town.

We found a nice restaurant, removed our coats and had a lovely lunch, we then rugged up again and went for a walk around this charming English village. We had time for a coffee before heading back to start week two of classes at 5.00 pm, and we found a table at the Yeoman's Tearooms, where once again we took off our coats. We were both gobsmacked to find a bigger than usual white feather stuck on my sleeve, which had not been there between lunch and our walk. Sam was clearly enjoying the trip as much as we were!

Our second course saw Sandra and I in different classes and this was perfectly fine, because by this stage I was feeling so much stronger emotionally. I was ready to finally find out once and for all if I was a medium or not. During the first week I successfully completed many exercises, including readings of a psychic nature. In these readings I would blend my energy with a fellow class member's energy, and would be able to describe accurately things about them, their surroundings at home and their family.

I was thrilled by my positive results, but I was yet to be tested to see if I could make contact with the spirits belonging to these complete strangers. Sensing spirit is one thing: being able to share valid and factual information from the afterlife is quite another.

As I said earlier, for all of my life I had been acutely aware of sensing spirit around me. I actually thought everyone could feel this, but apparently this is not the case! It was in a class given by another wonderful tutor, Sandie Baker, that I successfully attempted my first one-on-one reading. I was teamed up with a lovely American woman called Jayme, who was to do a mediumship reading for me and then vice versa. Jayme had done this successfully many times before. I can't remember which of my loved ones she brought through – it wasn't Sam – but I do recall it was a very accurate reading and I enjoyed it very much.

When it was my turn, I did as I was instructed and got myself 'into the power'. I was then to just start talking about what I could feel, see, smell, sense or hear. We were also told, thankfully, that it may just feel like our own imaginations but to nevertheless go with whatever was being given. I could actually see a man's face. He was wearing a cap and I started to tentatively tell Jayme everything I saw or felt.

I was shown a picture in my mind of this man and Jayme: they were fishing in silence and enjoying the experience of just being together. I shared this with Jayme, and she said I was correct! I was absolutely elated, but still so nervous.

I asked silently within my head for more information, and next I saw a red-coloured dog. According to Jayme the man apparently had one of these, so I just kept on going. The next image was of this man sitting on a closed-in porch that had chairs and a small table on it. A cat slept on one of the chairs totally unfazed by many other dogs, including the red one. Jayme was just as thrilled as I was, as this porch had been built by the man's own hands and he was so proud of this achievement. He indeed also owned a gutsy old cat that slept among the dogs on the porch.

A random cob of corn was shown to me and so it went on. I won't go through the entire reading, but it was the most exciting thing I had ever attempted to do in my life. In the debrief afterwards Jayme explained that this man was her uncle, who had lived in the cornbelt area of America. They loved to fish together whenever they caught up with one another. It was always done in silence, as it was more about being together than having a conversation, and this was very much the feeling I was being given when I saw them fishing together. I had not been able to get the man's name or the uncle connection, but it turned out his name was Jim, my own dad's name! What a perfect outcome for my first reading.

I left the class feeling totally elated and couldn't wait to share my fantastic breakthrough with Sandra at coffee time. She was also having wonderful success with her own readings, and we both knew without a doubt that we had made the best decision of our lives to be at this incredible place of knowledge and teaching.

A day later, I entered a beautiful room that was new to me. It was called the Blue Lounge. This was my first class with a wonderful and funny Scottish tutor, Thelma Francis. I walked into the circle and chose a random chair and sat down. Right there in front of me was a lovely little white feather marking my spot. I picked it up and put it with the others I had been collecting that week. Sam was right there with me, just as this new class about demonstrating mediumship was about to begin.

I believe Sam came to me at this time to give me the confidence to put my hand up and give this new and totally daunting exercise a go. After watching Thelma perform an amazing display of what's called 'platform mediumship', she then asked for a volunteer to do a demonstration. I sat there experiencing a massive internal argument raging in my head about me coming all this way to England and how the opportunity was right there, right now. I'd paid all this money to be there, and I would kick myself when I got home if I didn't at least try, and so it went on.

The next minute, I looked at my right hand and it was hanging awkwardly in mid-air; I swear it was not me who raised it! Thelma was thrilled to have a so-called volunteer, and when I stood beside her she asked if I had done much demonstrating. I had barely seen it done, let alone ever taken part as the medium. When I said as much, she gave me a very hopeful 'Well, this will be interesting.'

Once again, I won't give a blow-by-blow account of everything that took place, but I will share some of it with you as it was such a powerful happening for me and also highly emotional for both myself and everyone there.

With encouragement from Thelma I got into the power, and within seconds saw as plain as day a young boy aged about twelve years old. Unlike with a one-on-one reading, where it is just that, with demonstrating it is up to you as the medium to connect the spirit with a recipient in the room. To do this you must extract, decipher and deliver the information being given to you from the spirit world. It all sounds perfectly straightforward on paper!

Through telepathy with this lovely young spirit, we started to communicate with one another. I asked the boy how long ago he had passed into the afterlife, and I somehow received the words 'thirty years'. I shared this information with the blank faces before me; I clearly needed more than this tiny scrap of information to make a firm connection with the right person. I enquired to see the boy's family, then I saw his mum and dad and two other children, a brother and a sister, and he went and stood in the middle of his siblings. This finding was shared also, but there were still no responses from the class. I must have been looking desperate by now, but Thelma continued to offer gentle encouragement and urged me to ask more questions of my twelve-year-old spirit.

I asked where he had lived and to be shown these environs, then I saw a nice house in the country and some farm animals. Strangely, only one of each: one cow, one sheep, one chicken and so on. To me this meant it was more of a hobby farm and not a big working farm. At this point, a lady at the back of the room raised her hand and said she had a childhood friend who had passed away about thirty years ago and he lived on such a farm.

Thelma told me I had my contact and I was to direct everything from now on to that woman and not to the others in our class. I saw the boy disappear and then walk back to where I could see him. He was carrying a ball and playing with it, and I felt he had had a happy childhood and this was his way of showing me. The next minute he disappeared again, and this time he appeared wheeling a bicycle past me. At this point I felt extremely ill and very emotional. I said that I felt he had been killed on his bike. With this, the lady at the back of the classroom started to cry.

Thelma was trying to keep me on track, wanting to know what else I was getting. I was shown the horrific pain experienced by his family after learning that their young son had passed away, and when I tried to express this all I could see was our own pain and desperation after hearing of Sam's passing. I became very emotional. I had practically everyone in the room in tears, and this is definitely not what a good medium is supposed to achieve.

I was finally able to continue, and Thelma asked me to enquire why this boy had come through today. He appeared before me wearing a school uniform and he was in a classroom. He was smiling and looked so happy. His message was that he could not complete his own education, which he had enjoyed so much, and he wanted my recipient to continue with her own studies into mediumship because it was so important that she do this. All of a sudden he was gone, the energy changed and there was no more contact.

In the debrief immediately afterwards, I was told that this was a childhood friend of my classmate and they had both grown up together in Holland. He was indeed the middle child, living with his family on a small farm, and he was twelve years old when he passed after being accidentally hit on his bike by the midwife who had brought him into the world twelve years previously!

It was such a tragic story, but I was elated that this beautiful young soul in the spirit world had chosen me to come to and that I was able to feel his presence and deliver his evidence of survival to his old friend. His name was Jos. I can't remember the Dutch lady's name, but I do remember we both hugged and cried afterwards.

Through Sam, Dad and the greater spirit world, I had all the confirmation I needed to know that this path was going to very much be the direction of my focus into the future. I had finally found my place again in life. Yes, I was a very late starter, but I know now that I was never meant to fully discover my amazing gift of mediumship any earlier. It came to me exactly when I needed it to, allowing me to actually feel that I was finally starting to heal, bit by bit every day, and I could now help others do the same.

Each and every day thereafter at the college, I was able to accurately read for class members in all of the lessons we were asked to complete.

It absolutely felt so right and it was amazing to be able to describe strangers' loved ones, their personalities and past experiences jointly shared with the numerous spirits who had made themselves known to me.

Somehow, friendships made at Arthur Findlay College are so deep and heartfelt. We are all there for a variety of reasons, and without a doubt many like myself attend because they have had such tragic personal losses in their lives. Most simply want and need to find answers about where their loved ones have gone and to know if they are okay. This common bond certainly made for easy conversation, both in and out of class, and it's wonderful to still be in touch with everyone via Facebook and occasionally in person.

Sandra and I had one last stopover on our way home to Australia, in Dubai with Lorraine and Graham. Lorraine and I were great mates from Mooroopna High days, and she was kind enough to collect us literally in the middle of the night from Dubai's massive airport. We went home for a few hours sleep and then had three fun-packed days in Dubai, a new holiday destination for both of us.

Sandra and I had our own bedrooms during the stay, and on day one as I was plugging my phone into the charger I discovered a little white feather on the floor by the bed. How brilliant was this: Sam was still present and he was also sharing this next exciting destination with me. I mentioned my find to Lorraine, and she assured me that she had vacuumed the day before and there was nothing in the bedding that contained feathers. Perfect!

Lorraine and Graham were lovely hosts, although sadly Graham was rarely at home as he is a captain with Emirates airlines and had daily local flights to make. Lorraine was wonderful in showing us around their adoptive home of the past nineteen years, and with her vast knowledge of the city it was like being shown around by a local.

Just as when reconnecting with Helen and David, it was so wonderful to be with my old school friend Lorraine. I had not met Graham before, but it was one of those experiences where you just feel that you already know someone, and our time in Dubai was extremely special. I feel so blessed that this trip was such a success on every level possible.

Incredibly, Sandra already knew Lorraine from their childhood days as Brownies in Tatura, and they had also apparently played tennis together on Saturdays. The real clincher was that Lorraine's father, Frank, had for years managed an orchard belonging to John Cornish, who just so happened to be Sandra's uncle! Tatura was also where Lorraine had been born and raised and yet here we were, us three country girls, halfway around the planet, reminiscing and having the time of our lives all together. How tiny this world really is.

Sandra and I arrived back in Australia, and to our respective homes in two different states, on 12 March 2015, both forever changed as people but in the most positive of ways possible. We have only seen one another once since our incredible adventure, but our connection runs so much deeper than needing to see one another in person. We communicate very regularly on Facebook and via email, and I truly feel that we are never far away from one another.

It pleased me so much that Sam's twenty-second birthday was celebrated as planned, with some of his wonderful friends at a local hotel. I was incredibly happy to be back home to share this night with

Sergio, Carla, Sam's mates (who are now ours) and, of course, with the unseen guest of honour himself, Sam!

Myself and Sandra at Arthur Findlay College in the United Kingdom, 2015

Clockwise from top right:
Lorraine, Graham and me in Dubai, 2015; me, David and Helen in Standlake, UK, in 2015; Sergio, me and Jordan in London, 2015; Seb, me, Brigitte, John and Matt in London, 2016

CHAPTER 16

The importance of celebrating birthdays and anniversaries

At first, as every significant milestone neared, it was always initially approached with total apprehension, verging on dread, but we all really wanted to continue having birthday parties for Sam. We also wanted to acknowledge the anniversary each year of the passing of all three boys.

Our first Christmas was by far the hardest one. I had not been looking forward to the day at all, as it was normally such a wonderful and fun celebration and I knew that this one would not be that. Carla was still away in Europe with Paul, so it was just Sergio and me arriving at Robert and Nadine's to join their girls and the rest of the Alderuccio family. It felt so utterly lonely.

Our last Christmas together, 2011

It was difficult to not reminisce on the Christmas before, where we had a full and complete head count from our family, and life seemed totally uncomplicated and carefree.

After lunch Nadine and I talked about Sam, and I shared with her our stories about finding small white feathers courtesy of him. She was genuinely amazed and I'm sure also slightly sceptical, although she was kind enough not to show this. The next day I received a phone call from Nadine to let me know that after we went home, as she was dismantling the tables, she noticed a small white feather fall to the floor. I think that this made Nadine's Christmas extra special as well; she was now seeing for herself the wonders of what was possible, as opposed to what was perhaps only in my imagination.

Sam has truly never left us, just as we would never leave either of our children. We are meant to be together, and through our somewhat unusual form of communication I know that we still actually are as one.

In a joint decision between all three families, we wanted to recognise, acknowledge and honour the first anniversary of the boys' passing. Months beforehand we decided that it was our combined wish to mark 3 May 2013 with a big private picnic in the local park, very near to the accident site on Westgarth Street. On this day we would also jointly plant a new tree, courtesy of the local council, to replace the charred stump that had recently been removed.

We all worked closely together with the local council and with one another, to make the day as uplifting as possible for everyone present and to celebrate and remember the short lives of our three beautiful sons. The police cordoned off the road for the duration of the tree planting, and each parent and sibling released various coloured balloons into the heavens for the boys. Sam's were red, the colour of his tee shirt he wore on that fateful day.

None of us really knew what to do to mark this ominous date, but doing nothing at all seemed very disrespectful to all of the boys, as well as to their many, many friends. Words were said by representatives of each family and music was played to the gathering of a few hundred close family and friends. Delicious sandwiches were enjoyed, thanks to Raph's wonderful family, and tears were shed and more stories told.

Many of us dispersed afterwards, as a huge collective group, to the Terminus Hotel in Clifton Hill, where lots of separate toasts were made, more tears were shed and, thankfully, much laughter could also be heard. It was actually a wonderful day and evening, and I think that we all felt so much better for honouring our sons in this way.

Sam's twentieth birthday was ten months after the accident, and a wonderful and thoughtful gathering was arranged by Sam's old boss, Peter, from Amigos. Sam worked at two different Amigos venues, ours in Hardware Lane and another one with different owners in Carlton. Peter had since opened an Amigos on Brunswick Street, Fitzroy and the birthday catch up was to take place here, with Peter hosting it. It was a lovely and kind thing to do and we were all very appreciative.

It was so heart-warming to experience the kindness of friends, to randomly do such lovely and considerate things. We invited a small bunch of Sam's closest friends to come along, and we asked some family members as well. I remember catching the tram from our city venue to Peter's Amigos, and as I got off I saw two of Sam's best friends from Wesley, Andy and Andrea, carrying a huge painting of Sam riding on an elephant. This immediately brought me to tears, as it was obviously and unbeknown to us copied from a photograph taken in Thailand, on his dream trip away with school friends that included Andy and Andrea.

They both proudly presented the painting to Sergio, Carla and me, and it now takes pride of place in our bedroom. Each morning I look at it, and the way it sums up Sam's essence truly makes me smile. Sam is sitting astride his favourite animal, the elephant, giving everyone two thumbs up and wearing the broadest of cheeky smiles. Often when I am feeling down and in need of a pick me up, I look at this painting and give him the thumbs up back! Somehow this makes me feel strangely buoyed in some way.

After having beautiful food and drinks at Peter's, we joined the youngies present for more birthday drinks at the Evelyn Hotel, also on busy Brunswick Street. The pub was absolutely packed, and all of these gorgeous young people kept saying hello to us and giving us hugs and kisses. We soon discovered there was a separate party happening, also in Sam's honour, for his birthday. Totally amazing in every way. I was now finally getting my head around the difference between a 'gathering' and a 'party'; we had just gone from one to the next!

Sam's twenty-first birthday was always going to be such a tough decision, regarding what we would do to celebrate. Large or small? Family or friends or both? Hotel or restaurant? Do we, or don't we?

Eventually, after looking at a variety of local pubs near Flemington, because after all that was where Sam had grown up, we decided to book the Leveson hotel in North Melbourne. According to some local mates Sam had enjoyed the odd beer there, so it just seemed right.

The function room at the rear had a great courtyard, with a retractable Perspex ceiling and plenty of indoor space, and huge bi-fold doors to open things up beautifully. We made the booking, and I remember writing a tearful email from our office at Amigos explaining that the guest of honour would not actually be noticeably present on the day. I received a heartfelt response from the function manager, who was also a mother, and I sensed from her beautiful words that she had also shed a tear when our booking was confirmed.

It was decided by the three of us that Sam's party was going to be really memorable, and we wanted all of Sam's friends attending to take home a reminder of him from the party. After Sam passed away, a wonderful friend called Charlie, who attended Xavier College, completed two massive and legal graffiti pieces in Sam's honour. One was in Flemington, on a long timber paling fence beside the railway line, saying 'RIP Clerks'. The other beautiful graffiti mural was on the back of Lorenzo's garage in Toorak, also facing the train line, and it said 'RIP Da Vinci'.

Sam's mates at the piece on Lorenzo's garage

Sam would have loved the positioning of both stunning pieces, and we are very grateful to Charlie for painting them and to the council for allowing the one on Lorenzo's garage to stay. Sadly, the Flemington tribute was removed by the local council after much pressure from aggrieved locals. I totally appreciate that Sam's graffiti antics ruffled many feathers, but at the time it seemed very insensitive to us that this beautiful tribute had to be removed. We were so grateful, however, when the local council professionally photographed the artwork and gave us two framed photos of Charlie's wonderful tribute.

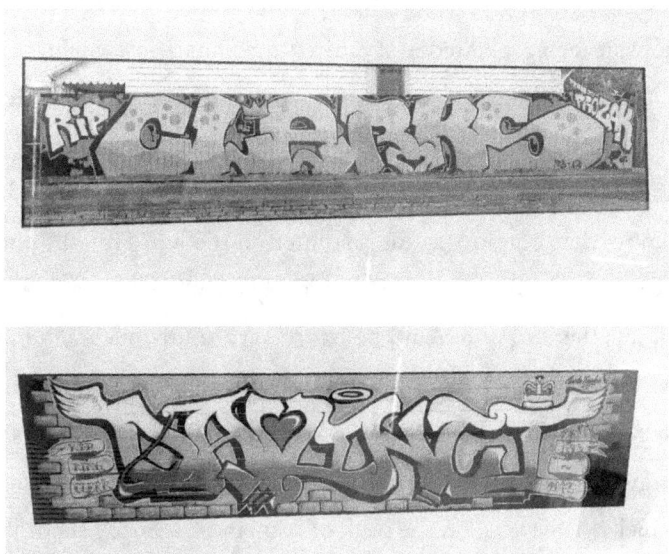

Because of the years of birthday parties, general celebrations and just regular childhood play time at our local neighbourhood park, we really wanted to honour Sam in some way that would have a lasting reminder of him, attached to both the park and also to the neighbourhood in which he grew up.

Sergio approached the local council to ask about the possibility of us planting a tree in the park in Sam's honour, and they kindly not only allowed this to happen, but also provided a huge boulder to which we could attach a plaque. A lovely native bottlebrush tree was planted beside it, also a gift from the Moonee Valley Council. We will always be so very grateful to then-mayor Jim Cusack for arranging all of this and making our personal tribute to Sam possible.

Even though I was happy and proud that a tree and subsequent plaque were being planted and erected for Sam, I just could not face being there on the morning that the arborist planted it. We had all been rung and invited to witness its planting, but I quite simply could not do it.

I know that Sergio was disappointed in me and I'm still not sure what Carla made of my no show, but lovely Billy, Sam's neighbourhood friend, was there to watch and he has so very kindly made it a mission of his ever since to check on the growth and well-being of Sam's tree, and to go there on special occasions to have a quiet drink with his mate.

Sergio arranged for a professional photograph to be taken of the 'Da Vinci' masterpiece on the back of Ann and Lorenzo's shed, and we had it screen printed onto black tee shirts to be handed out at Sam's twenty-first birthday party. We also added a small drawing of a family of four elephants, to depict our family, to the upper back of the tee shirts. This was Carla's design, and it is beautiful and very fitting. The adult elephant is leading a little one, which is holding the parent's tail with its trunk, then another adult is holding the little one's tail, followed by another small elephant that is holding that parent's tail. It illustrated our family perfectly.

I really wanted to include a special message with each of these wonderful tee shirts. I wasn't happy with just giving everyone one; more had to be said, but I didn't know what. A thought was brewing in my mind. I could feel it developing and growing but nothing was clear to me just yet, and time was running out as the party was only a week away. On my day off I drove down to our local Officeworks on Alexandra Parade, and took with me a photo memory stick, an unformed idea and not much else.

The first thing I did was to find the photographic section, to go through the photos on the memory stick. This was totally overwhelming and I was trying to cry discreetly, so no one would notice me. Eventually I chose a lovely photo of Sam taken on his last Christmas Day.

Sam, Christmas Day, 2011

It was all too much; what was I supposed to do now? I had no idea, so I printed off just two A5 size photos and retreated back to the car, having achieved nothing at all other than having a mini, albeit discreet, breakdown in our nearby Officeworks store.

The strangest thing happened next. As I was about to turn the key in the ignition and drive home feeling utterly defeated, I felt this enormous feeling of strength wash over me and I marched straight back into Officeworks and headed for the stationery section. I was on auto pilot; someone unseen was guiding me to complete the next steps and I didn't dare question what those steps were.

I bought a packet of one hundred A4 pieces of nice thickish paper and a texta pen that had a good steady flow of ink to it. I sat quietly in a corner of God knows where and proceeded to write a note from Sam to his fellow party guests; it went as follows.

13/3/14

My gift from me to you. Wear it with a smile and remember our happy times together. See you again on the flip side. Love Sam (D.V) XXX

I'm not sure exactly where those words came from, but they seemed perfect. I had written 'Sam's words' on both the left- and right-hand sides of the paper one hundred times. On reflection, I should have just bought a smaller page size, and I would only have had to write it once and had them all photocopied!

Clear thinking was not a strength on that day. I went to the young man who operated the guillotine and had the pages all cut evenly in half. I really can't imagine what he was thinking as he read Sam's words, written in my hand, but he certainly was extremely polite and probably just hoping that this emotional-looking wreck of a woman would vacate his place of employment very soon. Next stop was back to the photo man, where I had two hundred photographs printed the same size as the notes. Back I went to the car feeling like a different person.

It was an incredible experience and none too subtle on Sam's part. My actions were totally being driven by someone else, to do what I did. I came home and rolled all the tee shirts up according to their various sizes, glued the photo to 'Sam's note', put a hole in the corner and tied each one with string, making lovely packages to hand out as everyone arrived to greet us at the party. It was truly a joint effort, with Sam directing the process, as I had absolutely no idea where to start.

Sam's twenty-first birthday party was a beautiful affair, and I know for certain that many of his friends were wondering what the heck the vibe would be on the day. Was it going to be a hideously sad day of family and friends mourning Sam's physical absence, or a day that was a real twenty-first birthday party and subsequent celebration? Thankfully, it was the latter.

As requested by us, many friends brought along photographs of themselves with Sam, and these all went up onto pinboards purchased on another more emotionally stable trip back to Officeworks. Sergio and Carla made beautiful speeches to and about Sam, and various friends, both of our vintage and Sam's, stood and spoke heartfelt words to their dear friend, our son. I could only manage to applaud each speaker and raise my glass to my darling boy. It was both so happy and, yet, so very sad.

The tee shirts were given out to each guest on arrival, after a very fast assessment of body size. Everyone was so surprised to be receiving a gift, photo and note from Sam, and all showed pure emotion and joy at the gesture. As the day progressed, more and more young ones disappeared into the loos and came out wearing their Da Vinci tee shirts. It was wonderful to see, and it made us all so very happy to witness them, as a united group of beautiful friends all celebrating the short but exuberant life of their mate, Sam.

Charlie, me and Sergio at Cafe Trutrack celebrating Sam's birthday

It was now our turn to receive a gift, and we were presented with a parcel wrapped in paper that had been signed by many of Sam's friends attending the party. Inside was a very large black square of heavy duty mesh, the sort used on building sites to prevent people from entering the workplace. As we unfolded the mesh we could see it had been tagged by the now infamous lover of graffiti, Clerks! A friend of Sam's called Romy had seen the signed mesh on a building site and had begged the workman to let her have it, after somehow explaining to them the importance of having it as a gift for Sam's twenty-first birthday. It was a beautiful gesture and I do treasure having this to keep tucked away, together with so many other keepsakes relating to Sam.

We continue to celebrate all of Sam's birthdays, this year and last, we had his twenty-third and twenty-fourth celebrations with his wonderful friends at Cafe Trutrack in Leveson Street, North Melbourne. It's owned by a good friend of ours, another Sam; there must be something about the name that makes people so lovely. I have never, ever been disappointed by a single Sam I have met.

Each year I always like to post a birthday wish on Facebook to remember and acknowledge Sam's birthdays. It may seem odd to some, but to me it's all very much a part of keeping Sam so very present in our lives and in the lives of his many, many friends, and also his extended family. Please don't mistake this gesture with me being delusional, or in some sort of chronic denial. I am painfully aware that Sam has departed this world for the next, but his memory still lives on. Sam is now in spirit and, like all spirits, he still deserves to be honoured.

Below are my Facebook messages from his twenty-third and twenty-fourth birthdays. I just wanted to share these brief and heartfelt messages with you.

2016

Happy 23rd birthday our dearest Sam.

March 13 will always be 'your' day, your special date. It is a day that will always be remembered and celebrated by us, your extended family and by your many, many friends.

We have all aged over the last 4 years and your friends have grown from teens to adults, and I always still picture you among them standing tall, fair and handsome with that smile of smiles ...Love, like life never dies, our love for you is ever lasting, from here to eternity.

Keep sending your signs and messages darling Sam, they make us smile and the happiness they bring is immeasurable.

Sending so much love, Mum, Dad and Carla xxx

2017

I struggle every year with knowing what to write, what to say to honour our beautiful Sam, who today, if he were physically present, celebrates his 24th birthday. To me, he is very much still with us, but now in spirit only. Happy birthday our darling boy, you always had the most amazing ability to make others feel happy, worthy and proud … it's actually a rare gift and certainly never a given that any of us will ever feel this way. Today we honour you Sam and remember all that you gave to us in your very short, but carefully crafted lifetime. You were here for a reason and you certainly succeeded in touching more lives than we will never truly appreciate. Happy birthday Sam, Sam A, Da Vinci, Clerks, Buddy, Mate ... we all have a special place and name for you that lives on in our hearts. Much love, from Mum, Dad and Carla xxx

Sam's birthday celebrations were an opportunity for Sergio, Carla and I to get together and share this special day, this important date, with Sam's amazing friends. It's funny and may even appear quite odd to some, but we now no longer even include any family or friends from our 'vintage' at Sam's birthday gatherings. They have somehow become a very special day where just us three, Carla's boyfriend, Paul, and all the youngies get together to celebrate Sam's life and what he meant and continues to mean to everyone. The stories are priceless, and because it's just us and them we all seem to come together with total ease and we absolutely love it!

There are some things I just cannot and will not change. Whenever I sign a birthday, Christmas, christening, sympathy, wedding, engagement or any other kind of significant card at all, I quite simply cannot bring myself to not include Sam's name in the sign off. The only exception to this is if Sam never knew the recipient or vice versa. I've never truly understood what the cut-off time is, to cease including your offspring living or otherwise on written correspondence, but I will always sign off with 'Kerry, Sergio, Carla and Sam too'. He deserves the recognition, and will always be that fourth family member no matter how many years go past.

Prior to Sam's passing, I was always happy, eager even, to be asked by complete strangers who I had just met to talk about my family. Invariably, the 'How many children do you have and what are they doing?' question would be asked, and I was always more than pleased to share that we had two lovely kids, both were great and they were studying, travelling, working or whatever was going on in their busy lives.

After 3 May 2012 I totally dreaded meeting uninformed newcomers, for my sake and theirs, I hoped that this question would not be asked. I would actually consider my answer in advance, as I instinctively knew that I couldn't avoid the inevitable forever. Would I say that we only had one child, a gorgeous daughter, and then bang on interminably about Carla's many achievements, barely drawing breath and hoping they would regard me as 'hard work' and move on to someone else in the room? This was by far the easier option of the two, but I simply could not do this to Sam. How dare I suggest that he never existed and was not included in our family count of four?

Initially my answer was ever so difficult to voice, but at least it was honest. 'We have two children, a daughter Carla and a son Sam, who tragically passed away aged nineteen, in a car accident.' Responses always vary, depending on who you are sharing this news with, but I always feel better for being truthful about our situation. There have been times when I have found myself standing or sitting opposite a parent suffering a similar loss to ours, and there is always a deep sense of knowing; what passes between you is hard to explain, but it is so very evident to me and presumably to them.

CHAPTER 17

Where we are now

Only a few short years have passed since I joined my first circle group, early in 2014. It was here that I started to truly explore why I had always felt a little different to other people. When I look back now, I find it absolutely inconceivable what has transpired since then. When I do reflect, which is quite often, I gradually start to recall more and more unexplainable little things that have taken place throughout my lifetime, and I would like to share some of these here.

It really is difficult to know where to start with these memories, which at the time seemed perfectly normal, but on reflection there are many strange circumstances. Like everything in life everything happens for a reason, and I am still left in awe as to how these things are orchestrated.

I'm sure many of you have also experienced totally unexplainable situations, feelings and emotions, and often, for some strange reason, we never think more about it. I invite you to read my personal accounts and then reflect upon your own experiences; I'm sure some similarities will be there.

On 3 May 1978 I was driving to my workplace at Shepparton Preserving Cannery (SPC), in Shepparton, where I had been toiling as a factory worker since completing my Higher School Certificate the year before. I'm really not sure why I never had the desire or dream to attend university like so many of my friends. I seemingly just wasn't wired that way.

The opportunity to start work during the busy fruit season was offered to me after I met the general manager of SPC over beers with friends one Friday night at the Victoria Hotel in Shepparton. It was a chance to make some money for myself before a 'real' job presented itself, and my parents were pleased to see me in the workforce only weeks after finishing high school.

I was apparently regarded as being a good and solid employee at SPC, as I was one of a few who were asked to stay on after the season was over to do menial tasks, like stencilling the cardboard boxes and other mind-numbing jobs. The people around me were lovely and always very pleasant, so as much as the physical work was terrible the working environment was not.

Because my autumn shifts started later in the day than when the fruit was being processed, I no longer needed to clock on at 7.00 am but at a later time mid-morning. I headed off in my low-slung Morris car towards Shepparton from our new family hobby farm in Toolamba, where we had moved to only two years previously after selling our modest weatherboard home in Tatura.

On the way, I saw an old high school friend called Jamie hitch-hiking in the direction that I was travelling. This is where the unexplainable happened. I normally would never pick up a hitch-hiker and I only did so because I knew him. We had gone to Mooroopna High together, and my dad and Jamie's had also completed some joint work projects together over the years.

It was only because I had Jamie in the car with me and we were talking that I didn't look in the direction of the construction site where my wonderful dad was working, just as I normally did. I drove past the building site every weekday in the main street of Mooroopna, and without fail would look in that direction, simply because I might get a glimpse of my dad from a distance.

Had I carried out my regular ritual I would have noticed a shocking scene of chaos, with police and ambulance vehicles in full view from the road and frantic movement everywhere. It was the day that my father and his workmate, Alastair, both perished in a horrible workplace accident.

Jamie was somehow 'sent' to me. He was my diversion, he was in my car on that very day at that very time for a reason. He had never been driving with me in the past and has never done so since. In fact, it was the first and last time I saw Jamie since we had left school the year before. It took me many decades to realise the true relevance of Jamie being there that morning.

There have been so very many signs and warnings throughout my lifetime, and it's only when I think back and question what they meant that it makes total sense to me now.

If we go back to that fateful day in November 1989 when Sergio and I had our full throttle encounter with a farm ute, a Harley-Davidson and the bitumen, a very strange thing happened just prior to the accident. We had stopped, as a collective group of HOG members, somewhere way out in the north-eastern suburbs for coffee prior to our country ride of only a few hours to Lake Eildon. We were certainly not hard-core bikies on any level; most were just Harley enthusiasts out for a regular Sunday ride.

Not long after we took off, a roaring convoy of twenty-five Harley-Davidson bikes (we were number twenty-one). I was sitting on the back behind Sergio, feeling relaxed and enjoying the scenery near Flowerdale, and somehow I felt the strap buckle on my denim bag come undone. I have no idea how it undid itself, as it was just around my body and hanging by my side. Nothing was applying any real pressure to the strap; it just gave way and became undone, but not broken.

The strange thing was that I was somehow able to grab it before it blew out behind me and hit the riders following us. Importantly, I went from being in a very relaxed state to being in a hyper alert one. Minutes later, I saw the ute carrying the farmer and his wife sitting facing in our direction, with the right blinker on to turn, presumably into the gateway of their property.

Clearly, the farmer had lost patience with waiting for all of the annoying motorbikes to clear the entrance to where they lived. He then decided to cut through motorbikes twenty and twenty-one in an attempt to get home faster. It was a near fatal mistake for us, especially as he then panicked and stopped the ute in our path.

I feel without a doubt I was being given a warning to be very alert right at that time, and I remember telling Sergio just before the crash that my handbag had broken and that I had just managed to grab it before it flew away. Sergio was now also very much in the present and very much aware of the impending crash.

Miraculously, he somehow managed to swerve the motorbike around the back of the ute and reduce our speed from 100 km/h to 90 km/h. It was enough to thankfully save our lives but not our left legs, which went snap, snap before we hit the roadway.

Fast forward to May 2012, just after Sam's passing. It was only days after the catastrophe and two beautiful friends, a mother and son called Jo and Sam, who I spoke about in an earlier chapter, came to visit us at Farnham Street. Jo and I were having a teary heart to heart over a glass of wine, when she started to tell me about her interest in metaphysics and how she had studied this subject in the past. To be honest, at the time I really had no idea what metaphysics was, but when Jo expressed her belief in the afterlife and knowing that we can never truly die she had my complete attention. We were on the same page, and she was not remotely alarmed when I told her that I felt Sam's presence on a daily basis, and also how I feel him comforting me.

Jo had experienced some amazing phenomena of her own over the years, but that is not my story to tell. As we chatted about my Sam, his passing, his life, his everything, the leather necklace I was wearing broke of its own accord and fell into my lap. Nothing was wrong with the necklace, and I certainly wasn't touching or pulling on it; it was just Sam's wonderful and unique way of letting us know that he was very much around and nothing was going unnoticed by him. We both just loved it!

Sam really seemed to have a thing for making contact via breaking my necklaces. There have been many occasions now, and I certainly never tire of it happening. On my first visit to Arthur Findlay College, I remember sitting and chatting to a lovely Irish woman called Trish, who I had befriended during the week. She was also a very loving mum, with two sons and a daughter. It obviously saddened her deeply when we were talking about Sam and his untimely passing. For those who know me, they would be very aware that I am never without a necklace of some description, or earrings, rings or bracelets for that matter!

This particular day, I was wearing a long piece of leather with about ten pearls randomly scattered along it. I wore it around my neck twice and there was absolutely no tension on it at all. As Trish and I spoke, I felt a slight tug on my necklace and I noticed that Trish was staring at it and looking quite dumbfounded. I glanced down to see that the leather had been pulled apart and it just hung there! It was totally amazing; I had not touched it all, nor had Trish. I knew it was Sam letting me know, us know, that he was there listening in and was enjoying the stories that we were sharing.

Sam is always very present when we are away overseas, and he has the most wonderful ways of letting me know that he is there. In 2014 Carla and I had yet another fantastic trip away together, this time to the USA. We had both been before but never together, and we were very excited to be having this joint experience at last. A few weeks before we left on our holiday, I had an extremely vivid dream. In this dream I was in New York and I was shopping in a wonderful bookshop that sold all of the things I now love and seek out. The shop in my dream was brimming with tarot cards and spiritual cards of all types, crystals, pendulums, jewellery, masses of self-awareness books and books of all types.

The shop conjured in my sleep appeared to be so vivid in both size and shape. I could see pendulums hanging in the back right-hand side of the shop, which were somehow swinging as they hung. I also saw certain books that I needed to purchase, but their titles were not shown to me. When I awoke this dream stayed with me, just as my dreams do when spirits have visited me.

After about five days in New York, I just knew I had to try to find the bookstore that was still so clear in my mind. I explained to Carla that I needed some 'me' time to explore a few special shops alone. She was extremely understanding of my newfound interest in the paranormal, mediumship and general weird stuff, but I also think she was slightly concerned and not altogether comfortable that I was seeking an unknown bookshop I had only seen in a dream! Talk about role reversals between family members.

We agreed that I would spend half a day doing my thing, then we would meet up again at 1.30 pm so we could have a late lunch and continue our exploring. I awoke that morning feeling so much anticipation and excitement about my new upcoming adventure. I was quite seriously heading off alone to find a bookstore in the vastness of New York City that I had dreamt about once, back in Melbourne, Australia!

Carla was understandably concerned about my lame-sounding plan, to somehow locate an unknown shop I had merely dreamt about. The night before my adventure, I once again consulted Google and found a bookshop called Namaste, about three kilometres from our Airbnb in

Nolita. This was where I was heading, for no other reason than the fact that it felt right.

I headed off on foot, another reason for Carla to fret, as I have never been that proficient at reading maps accurately. To make matters worse I didn't actually have a map, just the address of the Namaste bookstore some three kilometres away.

I followed my instincts and the vague memory of the Google map I had studied the night before. It took me about forty-five minutes to arrive at the street I was seeking. Amazing! I tentatively walked along it and found myself standing outside Namaste.

It honestly took me a few minutes before I could enter the shop, because I couldn't comprehend that I was about to somehow revisit my dream and be very much awake in it!

Just as I had envisaged, the front door to the shop was in the centre. I opened it and slowly entered, taking in all that I saw. Everything was there: the crystals, all of the huge varieties of spiritual cards and jewellery, books everywhere, masses of them. I acknowledged the greeting from the man behind the counter and slowly started to head towards the right-hand side at the back of the shop, in search of my swinging pendulums. I got halfway along and looked into a glassed cabinet to find a large display of pendulums in a petrified state of absolute stillness. I was heartbroken. The pendulums I had so vividly seen swinging in my dream were lifelessly dangling behind glass, doing nothing at all.

Forever the optimist, I decided to give up on my crazy notion that I had foreseen this day, this bookstore and the swinging pendulums, all of which seemed to have so much relevance in what I had experienced in my dream state. I would just buy a book or two instead, admit defeat to Carla and enjoy a good lunch together and another afternoon of shopping.

After passing the glassed cabinet I continued to the back right-hand corner, where I had seen the swinging pendulums in my dream, and lo and behold, there they were! There was another display of presumably cheaper pendulums, and they were gently rocking in the breeze of the air conditioning unit that was trying to combat the heat of summer in July.

Words cannot express what I felt then. I bought one of the pendulums to add to my growing collection, and I also bought a few new books, including a fantastic read called *My Son and the Afterlife* by Dr Elisa Medhus MD. When I was paying for my purchases, no doubt looking weirdly chuffed but unable to share my happiness with the man serving me, I noticed a small sign advertising mediumship readings on Wednesdays. What day was it? Wednesday, of course!

I enquired about availability and was told that the medium, Samuel (imagine that!), was usually fully booked. After a quick look at the bookings for that day, as luck would have it, or destiny in my case, Samuel just so happened to have an opening in thirty minutes. I had a quick coffee and then went to meet Samuel, the medium. It was a serviced office around the corner from Namaste.

Samuel, or Sam as he preferred to be called, was a lovely man who once worked in the movie industry designing theatre sets. I love creative types, so I was ready to hear whatever he had to say. My reading was only for thirty minutes, but he was ever so accurate. He talked about my mother's health issues at the time, my own on-going ear infection and the lingering jetlag that was still plaguing me weeks after landing in the United States. Finally we arrived at Sam, our Sam.

The car accident was described, including the fact that Sam was with others and not alone. He talked about how Sam had accidentally clipped a car and then hit a tree. It was all totally accurate and also amazing that the two Sams had clearly connected and could share with me what had happened. It doesn't seem to matter how many mediums you see, as long as the reading is accurate and honest the feeling of peace and hope that washes over you is both intense and lasting.

In my excitement in trying to get back to Nolita and Carla on time I inadvertently jumped on a train to New Jersey, which took the wind out of my sails somewhat. Through simple question asking of more savvy subway commuters, I managed to return to Manhattan and eventually to Carla. What a fantastic experience: I had actually dreamt about an unknown place and I was able to find it, and then have a truly wonderful mediumship reading as well!

I could write forever about the signs and messages that Sam has left for all of us, but that's not possible in this book alone. I would, however, like to summarise a few amazing things that happened on a trip to the UK with Sergio in 2015, to celebrate our twenty-fifth wedding anniversary.

As we typically do as a couple, Sergio and I often go our separate ways at times on holidays to ensure that both of us are having the experience we each want. On this occasion, Sergio went cycling in Corsica and the French Alps and I went to London for nine days to catch up with friends, explore previously unseen sites and just enjoy myself, which I certainly did. We were to then join up for a couple of nights in London and travel on to Scotland for a driving holiday and then down to the Lakes District and home.

I had been to London on a few occasions previously but had never stayed in the suburb of Shoreditch, which Carla had suggested to vary our perception that all of London is not like Chelsea and Kensington, where we normally stayed. Point taken! I found a flat in Shoreditch via Airbnb that had a proper security entrance and was on the first floor with a lift. Perfect.

As I always do pre travelling, I print off all of the relevant information with regard to getting to my various accommodation, booking receipts, pre-booked tours, travel tickets, vouchers and so on. I was feeling totally on top of things until my host at Shoreditch Airbnb, Kitty, altered our original plans to meet outside her flat and sent me information about alternative arrangements to collect the keys.

This was very last minute, and in my haste I had not printed off the new name or address from where I was to collect the keys. I somehow recalled the name of a quirky-sounding private club, something to do with a cow, but not much else. I had every other detail of our trip printed off except the fairly critical address for my accommodation for the next nine nights, until Sergio arrived. We always disengage our mobile phones when travelling so massive bills are not racked up, and I had no internet connection or way of contacting Kitty for more information.

After arriving at Victoria Street Station, I consulted my home-printed suburban maps and I was on my way. It was only then it became very apparent I had no idea where this private club was located.

After dragging my suitcase toward Shoreditch and asking many of the local traders about where I might find such a place, the answer was always the same: they all knew as much as I did.

By this stage, after flying for over twenty-six hours from Melbourne, I was both tired, anxious and on the verge of a major melt down if I couldn't find the street where the club and my flat key were waiting. I mentally gathered myself together and walked in the totally opposite direction to where I had originally been heading. I needed serious assistance, so I asked my dad and Sam to help me find what I was looking for.

After crossing a major road, I walked along for a block and then felt the need to cross over the street and turn right. At this juncture, I looked down and saw two small white feathers laying together side by side. I had my sign, my street and my belief, that all was well. After walking for only a few minutes I found the elusive club, and my key was waiting for me just as Kitty had promised. From here, I could follow my trusty hard-copy instructions to my new temporary London digs.

Sergio arrived nine days later, after his French cycling trip, and we had two terrific days in London together before taking a train up north to Edinburgh, our first taste of bonny Scotland. Sam was very much in feather mode on this trip, and they were prolific, timely and heart-warming to see.

On our first day out and about in London, we decided to have lunch near Mayfair at a Japanese restaurant, one of our favourite cuisines. We sat outside in the summer sunshine and I eventually required the bathroom, which was towards the back of this very smart-looking restaurant and then downstairs. When I came back up, there was a small white feather waiting for me near the top of the stairs. I went outside to our table and mentioned it to Sergio. He pointed to the ground near our table, where there were more feathers surrounding us. How fantastic!

On our second and last night in London, we met up with an old Wesley school friend of Sam's called Jordan, who was English and had spent two years at school with Sam while his family had a business posting to Melbourne. During my first week in London, Jordan had kindly Facebooked me to see if we could catch up. It had been about nine years since I had last seen Jordan, as a young thirteen year old, and I was ever so happy to hear from him and thrilled that he wanted to see us.

A venue and time to meet was decided, and off Sergio and I went to see Sam's old friend. We both just knew that Sam would have been incredibly happy that we were all having a night out together. I had walked the same route many times during the past ten days in Shoreditch, and the real estate business on the corner of our street and Brick Lane had always been open when I passed it by. Tonight, however, it was closed and they had pulled down all of their security shutters. Unbelievably, the entire shopfront was now a brightly coloured mass of feathers, all beautifully and professionally graffitied over the entire building!

Sam was clearly on to us, and as we continued on our way to meet Jordan we passed an art gallery that had a wall hanging in the window. It was made of masses of various feathers stitched onto a fabric backdrop in a lovely pattern and design. These feather sightings were all seen in the one day, and it was both feather overload and also very exciting.

We did catch up with Jordan and shared a fantastic night, sprinkled with funny stories, hugs and tears. Something about Sam had touched Jordan's soul, just as he had this effect on so many others in his short life, and we all felt so much better for catching up together.

After leaving lovely London for Edinburgh and other Scottish delights, we stopped for lunch one day in a small village. There were a couple of dining choices to choose from, but for some reason we chose an old-looking tearoom to quell our hunger.

There was an afternoon tea party taking place as we entered the charming old building, so we sat a little further back in another room where it was quieter. I could not believe my eyes when I computed that the rather garish wallpaper was actually pictures of large sets of feathered wings! If this wasn't enough, the woman who seemed to be the guest of honour at the tea party at the front was wearing a dress made of feather-patterned fabric! I have no answers as to how this could all be possible, but it was and we both felt perplexed and extremely happy about these none too subtle signs from Sam.

Sergio and me at the feather-laden cafe in Scotland in 2015

Sometime in 2015, I attended a psychic fair being held at the Coburg Town Hall. I went with a woman who was also attending my circle group at that time, and we strolled about looking at what was on offer in relation to various types of merchandise, different types of readings and so on. In the annexe area right outside the main hall some mediumship demonstrations were taking place, and we decided to sit in the audience to watch.

I remember my circle companion saying to me that if I was lucky, Sam might come through with a message from the other side. I can clearly recall thinking to myself that Sam would never make his presence felt at a public venue such as this one. Without wanting to sound too critical, the medium was making quite a sideshow out of his demonstration, and to me it went against everything that we had learnt at the college in the United Kingdom. This was not where Sam would want to be brought forward and have his messages conveyed.

I chose my words carefully and told my companion this, but in a much softer manner than I was thinking internally. Immediately, the necklace that I was wearing at the time, a small silver button on a short chain, just dropped off my neck and fell to the floor. We both saw it happen, and to me Sam was giving his verification that he would not be making an appearance that day via the medium in question!

My latest necklace incident was on 3 May 2017, on the fifth anniversary of Sam's passing. I have now returned to my old workplace at The Ark clothing company, where I worked prior to our buying Amigos. I am back working much more civilised part-time hours during the daytime. Amigos is now a silent partnership only, and my years on Hardware Lane are well behind me.

My shift that day at The Ark finished at 3.00 pm. It was the first day in five years I had worked on the anniversary of Sam's passing. For some reason, it just felt okay this year to do so. I left the store at Malvern and drove the 32 kilometres to Fawkner Crematorium, to take flowers to lay at Sam's burial site. It should have only taken fifty minutes in heavy traffic, and I thought I had plenty of time to get there before the gates closed at 5.00 pm.

I knew there was a flower shop not far from Fawkner and it was best to stop there, as I was also aware that the florist within the grounds was undergoing renovation. The traffic turned out to be extremely busy and I was becoming more and more stressed as I edged my way northward. I was also being very mindful that I may miss the opening hours. There is normally parking right outside the flower shop but, obviously, I had never been there mid-week after 4.30 pm. My regular parking space was now an operational laneway and clear zone to help cater for the constant flow of cars leaving the direction of the city.

To make matters worse, as I approached I could see in the distance the florist wheeling the last of the flower trolleys into the shop just before closing time. I put my left-hand blinker on and slowed down, just enough to mount the footpath without causing obvious damage to the car. I must have looked like a mad woman trying to re-enact a Starsky and Hutch manoeuvre on Sydney Road.

I cared not what anyone thought of me; I was on a mission to buy flowers and I was prepared to purchase a bunch of absolutely anything on offer.

The woman working there was lovely and I bought some bright yellow flowers for my boy. When I went outside to get back into our car, which was parked illegally straddling the footpath, I noticed that the long necklace I was wearing, which opens at the front, was totally undone and just hanging around my neck. It's such a tricky thing to open at any time, so I just put it over my head. I believe that Sam was thanking me for making such an effort to buy the flowers and to arrive before closing time on his anniversary. This made me cry and smile all at once.

***

Through Sam's untimely and unexpected passing, our lives are forever changed. For me, I have discovered a side that was always there, and I often wonder if I would have ever fully discovered my own gift of mediumship had Sam not passed away. I somehow doubt that I would have. I would have continued communicating with all of my loved ones in the spirit world, just as I always had, but I don't believe I would have ever learnt to use my skills properly, or know what I was capable of.

Through our own profound loss, I have found a part of me I am very proud of. I can now help other people to reconnect with their own loved ones, and the immense satisfaction this brings to me is impossible to fully express. I do think back often and remember how seeing Lorraine Culross changed our lives in such a positive way, and I would like to think I now do the same for others.

My readings are done at home on my days off, and I prefer to meet people through referrals only. At first it was a bit like me coming out of the closet, when telling old friends and new acquaintances what I do in my spare time. I am also very aware that not everyone agrees, believes or even approves of what I do as a medium, but it is not my job or role to change this.

Sam continues to guide me in so many ways, and all of them are always so very positive. I see the world through different eyes now; I am calmer, more compassionate to others, more interested in learning new things and opening my horizons to new experiences and possibilities. Very importantly, I feel I have still so much to live for.

Even though this book is in part about grief and coping with the loss of a young life, it hopefully is not a book that leaves you feeling empty, sad or without purpose or hope for the future. Sam's life with us was real. It was fabulous, it was something to remember fondly and often, which we all do. I prefer to embrace the memory of nineteen wonderful years together than to dwell on the years we all have to spend without him physically being here.

I choose to remember our son's amazing smile, his easy laughter, his funny comments and marvellous sense of humour, his compassion for others, his unconditional love and his more serious and caring side. We do get to choose what we remember, and I refuse to allow my grief to define me. Sam would never want that, and neither do I.

I wonder if inner strength can be passed on? I have often reflected on my own mother's way of coping with becoming a widow at only forty-four years of age. Resilience, thankfully, is a family trait, and now I know where mine comes from. My mother understandably became very restless after Dad's passing, and I believe that in her own way she was feeling very 'stuck' with her life and her lot.

Mum bought herself a failed guard dog, a Queensland blue heeler with the dubious name of Waggs. Waggs and I never hit it off, and it sadly remained like that for the remainder of her long life. Mum's next purchase was a Toyota four-wheel drive that she called Matilda, and a shot gun which to my knowledge remained nameless.

To Mum's credit she drove north-west, camping out by the side of the road with Waggs and her gun, lying close to Matilda. Her destination was a cattle station called Mount Doreen, in the middle of the Northern Territory, to take up her new temporary job as a cook for the stockmen. I've always admired her strength and tenacity to follow her heart and break all the norms and just do what felt right for her. Mum, I give you my heartfelt thanks.

In closing, I decided to include the words I wrote for Sam that my dear friend, Leanne, read on my behalf at Sam's memorial service. They very much seem to summarise the full, rich, happy and beautiful life that was our son's. These words are for you, my darling …

Written on Mother's Day, May 2012
WORDS FOR SAM

Writing these words has been the most difficult task that I have ever had to endure.

Where do I start, what do I say and how can I possibly say enough to capture all that Sam meant to me?

After days of being unable to write anything at all, I have decided to just write straight from the heart, as a Mother talking about her adored Son.

Some here today never had the pleasure of meeting Sam in person, so I would like to share his story ... our story.

Samuel James Alderuccio came into the world as an undiagnosed breach birth on Saturday, March 13, 1993 at the Mercy Hospital in East Melbourne. He arrived literally feet first, as if on a mission to start running and cram in as much as possible every single day.

Sam always had lovely manners and the ability to charm, so his first kind act was to have a gift wrapped toy waiting in his crib to present to his big Sister, Carla, just to get his life off to a good start back at Farnham St. A brilliant tactic on Sam's part and Carla loved her 'baby Sam' unconditionally thereafter.

In the past days, I have reflected on how lucky I was to have the opportunity to stay at home for the first nine years of Sam's life and eleven of Carla's. I got to share so much with them both and we had had a genuinely amazing time together.

We have been going back through our photo albums, and I am so pleased that we were are a family that got carried away with the holiday snap shots and photo taking in general. As you have seen here today from the photos that we have shared, Sam was a beautiful baby, a lovable kinder kid, a popular primary school student, a keen sportsman, a gregarious and loved secondary school mate, a loved work colleague and of course an adored Son, Brother, Grandson, Nephew, Cousin and friend to so many of you here.

Sam was busting to start kinder at St Brendan's in Flemington and he loved his time there and met so many wonderful friends, who he still kept in touch with til the end. It's hard for me to name only a few friends, as I don't wish to alienate others, but Sam O'Brien and Charlie Guthrie are stand out mates from kinder days. Inseparable, mischievous and gorgeous boys who rotated between one another's houses a few days and nights every single week, year in, year out.

From kinder, Sam went to Flemington Primary School, where his circle of friends grew and grew. He played footy, cricket, trumpet, guitar and sometimes the 'joker', however, everyone loved his cheeky outgoing nature. Sam was a class captain in Grade 6 and left Flemington Primary bound for Wesley College in St Kilda Road where Carla was already a student.

I will never forget Sam at the Orientation Day in mid summer, where he insisted on wearing the complete school uniform of shorts, socks pulled up, shirt, tie, jumper, blazer and shiny school shoes. No one else was wearing all of this on such a hot day and Sam never, ever managed to accomplish this standard of dress again, in all of his six wonderful years at Wesley.

Wesley College was never a challenge for Sam on a social level, he brought friends home from week one to stay and thankfully this never changed. The only factor was that they were rarely in singular lots, our boy preferred en masse.

Study was not a high priority in Sam's earlier education at Wesley, but footy and tennis were a real focus, as was building up a bigger and bigger friendship base ... smart move, my darling, it has served us well.

Sam worked incredibly hard last year in his VCE year to achieve the marks that he needed to study at Victoria University in 2013, after having a gap year in this one. Carla often joked that he crammed five and a half years of study into six months to get through, but he got there and this made us all so proud.

Travel has always been a huge priority in our household and our first overseas trip together was in 2000, for a three week trip to New Zealand. We had originally planned a road trip across America, but when we realised that the 'are we there yet?' question was being asked on the Western Ring Road, as we were leaving Flemington to see Nan and Pop in Mansfield, that the US would have to wait.

Sam and Carla loved travelling with Sergio and I and we just loved spending the time together, wherever in the world that we went. We were such lucky parents, as many teenagers are not wanting to continue with family holidays, however, Sam and Carla still loved travelling with us and were ready to go anywhere, at any time.

Some of our trips were done apart from one another in the past five years, because of Carla's study, including Sam and Sergio holidaying in Bali together, and with Sam and I having a ball in the US when he was sixteen. Carla and Sergio used to tease us unmercifully, about being such tourists and going to Disneyland, Universal Studios, riding roller coasters and visiting wax work museums in Las Vegas, going to Alcatraz in San Francisco and having a day of 'culture' in New York.

Sam and I knew how we both worked and happy compromises were always possible with Sam. Our day of culture in New York, meant that I had two hours at the Frick Gallery, with Sam spending the last hour of the visit patiently waiting on the steps outside, playing 'Snake' on my phone, and then four hours together at Ripley's Believe It or Not, on Broadway. The perfect day out in every way!

Last September, Sam, Jingles (his cat) and I spent a fantastic week at Apollo Bay, so Sam could prepare for his VCE exams. Sam had a study plan and a goal in mind that week and he ticked every box, in what he was hoping to achieve. Spending that week together was so enjoyable and I also loved listening to Bliss n Eso on his iPod on the drive home, and he also indulged me with a bit of Eminem, who I happen to love ... Another story of many that Sam and I shared.

January this year saw Sam head off without us in tow, to visit Thailand with six of his best friends, both boys and girls from Wesley. He absolutely loved this holiday and said that he was at his happiest at this time. Sam was due to team up with Caulfield and Jeremy for another trip this October to South America, but sadly they will be taking only wonderful memories of Sam with them instead.

We as a family are totally devastated at the sudden loss of our darling Sam, who had grown into a beautiful, kind and caring young man, with so much to live for. What I have just shared with you is only a tiny snap shot of who Sam was and what he meant to me and my family.

I read some words a few days ago that someone had left on a 'comments' page in the newspaper and a girl said that Sam had 783 Facebook friends and same in real life.

My darling Sam, I do believe in eternal life and knowing this gives me some peace.

Until we meet again ...

Mum xxxx

'The Unfinished' (author unknown)

Do not judge a biography by its length,
Nor by the number of the pages on it.
Judge it by the richness of its contents
Sometimes those unfinished are among the most poignant
Do not judge a song by its duration
Nor by the number of its notes
Judge it by the way it touches and lifts your soul
Sometimes those unfinished are among the most beautiful
And when something has enriched your life
And when its melody lingers on in your heart
Is it unfinished?
Or is it endless?

Alderuccio's, Christmas Day, 2017

Sam's 21st birthday at the Leveson hotel in North Melbourne, 2014

Sam at Amigos in Hardware Lane, 2012

Me and Sandra leaving Sydney for Arthur Findlay College in the UK, 2015

Sam in Daylesford with his faithful friend

Me, Billy, Dan and Gussy, together for Sam's birthday, 2018

About the author

Kerry Alderuccio's introduction to all things of a psychic nature came to her relatively late in life. It was after the tragic loss of her adored nineteen-year-old son Sam in a car accident that she realised an instinct she'd always had might be something more profound.

Throughout her life, Kerry had always been aware of changes in the energy around her: as her loved ones gradually passed away, she always remained aware of their presence. She had naively assumed that everyone felt such things.

It was after Sam's untimely passing that Kerry decided to act on this instinct and look for answers as to where Sam was and how contact could be made. She began her mediumship studies at Arthur Findlay College in the United Kingdom, and her career in mediumship progressed quickly from there.

This is Kerry's first book and is the result of her desire to share her amazing story, her moment of truth and her hope that others may find answers and peace in her words.

www.ingramcontent.com/pod-product-compliance
Lightning Source LLC
Chambersburg PA
CBHW071613080526
44588CB00010B/1120